ARCHITECTURAL DESIGN

EDITORIAL OFFICES:
42 LEINSTER GARDENS, LONDON W2 3AN
TEL: 071-402 2141 FAX: 071-723 9540

EDITOR
Dr Andreas C Papadakis

EDITORIAL TEAM: Maggie Toy (House Editor), Vivian Constantinopoulos, Nicola Hodges, Helen Castle
DESIGN TEAM: Andrea Bettella (Senior Designer), Mario Bettella, Owen Thomas
SUBSCRIPTIONS MANAGER: Mira Joka, BUSINESS MANAGER: Sheila de Vallée

CONSULTANTS: Catherine Cooke, Terry Farrell, Kenneth Frampton, Charles Jencks, Heinrich Klotz, Leon Krier, Robert Maxwell, Demetri Porphyrios, Kenneth Powell, Colin Rowe, Derek Walker

SUBSCRIPTION OFFICES:
UK: VCH PUBLISHERS (UK) LTD
8 WELLINGTON COURT, WELLINGTON STREET
CAMBRIDGE CB1 1HZ UK

USA: VCH PUBLISHERS INC
SUITE 909, 220 EAST 23RD STREET
NEW YORK, NY 10010 USA

ALL OTHER COUNTRIES:
VCH VERLAGSGESELLSCHAFT MBH
BOSCHSTRASSE 12, POSTFACH 101161
6940 WEINHEIM GERMANY

CONTENTS

ARCHITECTURAL DESIGN **MAGAZINE**

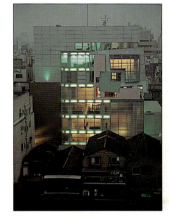

Peter Eisenman, Koizumi Lighting Studio

ARCHITECTURAL DESIGN **PROFILE** No 99

JAPANESE ARCHITECTURE II

GUEST-EDITED BY BOTOND BOGNAR

Bernard Tschumi, 'Le Fresnoy'

Shin Takamatsu, Syntax Building

BACK ISSUES

KISHO KUROKAWA

FROM METABOLISM TO SYMBIOSIS

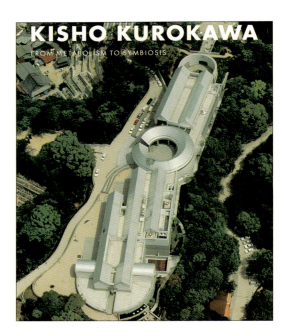

Kisho Kurokawa is one of the most prolific Japanese architects working today. This richly illustrated volume presents the full extent of his work all over the world, using analytical drawings showing the design process within the work, whilst Kurokawa's writings expound the theories which have influenced his architecture over many years.

Kurokawa traces his aesthetic and philosophical development from Metabolism, a movement which he founded in 1960, through Metamorphosis to Symbiosis, which he sees as the keynote of the nineties. These biological terms express the underlying themes of his work: adaptation and change, nervous systems, intermediate zones, ambiguity and hidden order – themes that are the characteristics of life itself. As society moves from the machine age to the age of life, these organic concepts become increasingly relevant. It is an age in which Japan, no longer dominated by the logocentric, binomial mentality of the West, will play an important part.

The work in this volume is presented in seven sections with projects spanning from the early Helix City plan for Tokyo, the 'Floating Factory' and Capsule Tower, to the more mature work of recent years such as the Sporting Club, Illinois; the Pacific Tower, La Défense, Paris; Melbourne Central; as well as the new wing to the Van Gogh Museum, Amsterdam.

The architecture of the future will embrace the past, and will value regional tradition; it will make use of the latest technology, but will bring out its human aspects: this is the architecture of Symbiosis, championed by Kisho Kurokawa.

305 x 252 mm, 312 pages, over 500 illustrations
ISBN 1 85490 119 2, HB £45.00
available from good bookshops worldwide

Published by

ACADEMY EDITIONS • LONDON

42 Leinster Gardens London W2 3AN Tel: 071-402 2141

THEORY + EXPERIMENTATION

AN INTELLECTUAL EXTRAVAGANZA

'Architecture', says Bernard Tschumi, 'is not about the conditions of design, but the design of conditions.' His words truly encapsulate the central theme of Theory + Experimentation: the liberation of architecture from long-established conceptions of propriety and functionalism (not to mention permanence) and its emergence as a free art of form and place. These events around the themes of theory and experimentation celebrate this process of artistic liberation and intellectual experiment.

Liberation might imply licence: the abandonment of the disciplined framework within which architecture has traditionally been practised, a lurch towards the arbitrary and the impractical – even the irrelevant. Yet it equally implies the reinstatement of architecture as an art, with the delicate balance between emotion and rationality at its core.

The recognition of the new electronic technology which has transformed the world in the last decade is another central element in the new architecture of freedom. There is the danger of a mere wallowing in the wonders of the electronic world, yet communications technology has changed the way in which humans address each other: architecture can no longer stand aloof from it but has to embrace it eagerly.

The relationship of the new architecture to the cherished roots of the Modern Movement is complex. Modernist architecture was serious, earnest, sometimes – alas – humourless. But the concept of architecture as the supreme art remained inviolate in the thought of Gropius, Corbusier and Mies. It is now being reinstated, after a period in which architecture went astray and became too often a mere branch of technology. Equally rooted in the classic period of modern architecture is the notion that architecture should be a pleasurable, even sensual, experience – as Zaha Hadid puts it: 'it gives you the idea of luxury. . .'

Architecture creates the new environment which Itsuko Hasegawa defines as 'second nature'. Her work is a specific response to the Japanese urban scene, with its terrifying rate of change and transformation. Architecture has become widely associated with the destruction of the natural world and with the dehumanisation of man. By placing man again at the centre, the new architecture is humanistic, enlightening, opening up new channels for the energies so often suppressed in a mechanistic society. In this sense, it is not elitist or specialist but essentially democratic. Coop Himmelblau pose the question: can architecture have relevance in a world of social and environmental chaos? Aren't there higher priorities? They answer that architecture can unlock the human spirit as no other art can. As the all embracing art of inquiry and discovery, it opens up new avenues to humanity and challenges every established way of thinking – and doing.

The Theory + Experimentation series of events show that far from being purely speculative or self-indulgently expressive, the new architecture is a challenge to conventional ways of life and work. It is offered as a major contribution to the continuing redefinition of architecture in a world of change. To speak of an international 'movement' would be a mistake – there is no set programme or ideology to which the participants conform – but there are the makings here of an architectural revolution which could affect the world as much as did the Bauhaus or CIAM. *Ken Powell*

Architects participating include:
Raimund **ABRAHAM**, Will **ALSOP**, **ARQUITECTONICA**, Günther **DOMENIG**, Peter **COOK**, **COOP HIMMELBLAU**, **DECQ** & **CORNETTE**, **DILLER** & **SCOFIDIO**, Peter **EISENMAN**, Mark **FISHER**, Itsuko **HASEGAWA**, **KRUEGER** & **KAPLAN**, Daniel **LIBESKIND**, **MORPHOSIS**, Eric Owen **MOSS**, Peter **PRAN**, Dagmar **RICHTER**, **STUDIO ASYMPTOTE**, Bernard **TSCHUMI**, Peter **WILSON**, Lebbeus **WOODS**, Zoe **ZENGHELIS**, Günther **ZAMP KELP**

Theory + Experimentation events include:
A **Conference** at the **Royal Institute of British Architects**; The **Academy Forum** at the **Royal Academy of Arts**; **The Annual Architecture Lecture** by Professor Bernard **Tschumi** at the **Royal Academy of Arts**; **Exhibitions** of architecture at the **Royal Institute of British Architects** and **Whiteleys**

ARQUITECTONICA
The relationship of Arquitectonica's work to the past or to place is oblique, more a metaphor or a nuance than a direct statement. Their work is the kind that often startles and shocks at first, buoyed by the kind of optimism that epitomised the Modern Movement: the belief that anything ought to be possible. It stretches both definition and reality.

Banque de Luxembourg

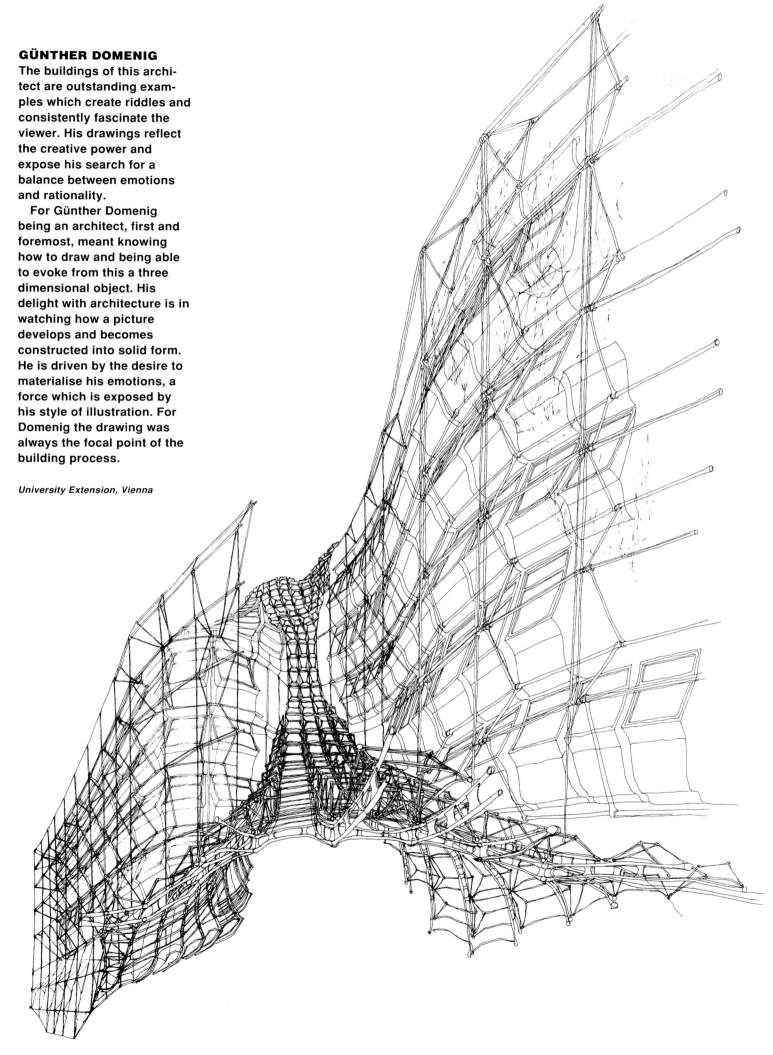

GÜNTHER DOMENIG

The buildings of this architect are outstanding examples which create riddles and consistently fascinate the viewer. His drawings reflect the creative power and expose his search for a balance between emotions and rationality.

For Günther Domenig being an architect, first and foremost, meant knowing how to draw and being able to evoke from this a three dimensional object. His delight with architecture is in watching how a picture develops and becomes constructed into solid form. He is driven by the desire to materialise his emotions, a force which is exposed by his style of illustration. For Domenig the drawing was always the focal point of the building process.

University Extension, Vienna

91 Ballhausplatz, perspektivische Darstellung der fallenden Tücher, der Fassade und der Membrane

PETER EISENMAN
Visions Unfolding:
Architecture in the Age of
Electronic Media

During the fifty years since the Second World War, a paradigm shift has taken place that should have profoundly affected architecture: this was the shift from the mechanical paradigm to the electronic one. This change can be simply understood by comparing the impact of the role of the human subject on such primary modes of reproduction as the photograph and the fax; the photograph within the mechanical paradigm, the fax within the electronic one.

In photographic reproduction the subject still maintains a controlled interaction with the object. A photograph can be developed with more or less contrast, texture or clarity. The photograph can be said to remain in the control of human vision. The human subject thus retains its function as interpreter, as discursive function. With the fax, the subject is no longer called upon to interpret, for reproduction takes place without any control or adjustment. The fax also challenges the concept of originality. While in a photograph the original reproduction still retains a privileged value, in facsimile transmission the original remains intact but with no differentiating value since it is no longer sent. The mutual devaluation of both original and copy is not the only transformation affected by the electronic paradigm. The entire nature of what we have come to know as the reality of our world has been called into question by the invasion of media into everyday life. For reality always demanded that our vision be interpretive.

How have these developments affected architecture?

Since architecture has traditionally housed value as well as fact, one would imagine that architecture would have been greatly transformed. But this is not the case, for architecture seems little changed at all. This in itself ought to warrant investigation, since architecture has traditionally been a bastion of what is considered to be the real. Metaphors such as house and home, bricks and mortar, foundations and shelter attest to architecture's role in defining what we consider to be real. Clearly, a change in the everyday concepts of reality should have had some effect on architecture. It did not because the mechanical paradigm was the *sine qua non* of architecture; architecture was the visible manifestation of the overcoming of natural forces such as gravity and weather by mechanical means. Architecture not only overcame gravity, it was also the monument to that overcoming; it interpreted the value society placed on its vision.

The electronic paradigm directs a powerful challenge to architecture because it defines reality in terms of media and simulation; it values appearance over existence, what can be seen over what is. Not the seen as we formerly knew it, but rather a seeing that can no longer interpret. Media introduce fundamental ambiguities into how and what we see. Architecture has resisted this question because, since the importation and absorption of perspective by architectural space in the 15th century, architecture has been dominated by the mechanics of vision. Thus architecture assumes sight to be pre-eminent and also in some way natural to its own processes, not a thing to be questioned. It is precisely this traditional concept of sight that the electronic paradigm questions.

Sight is traditionally understood in terms of vision. When I use the term 'vision' I mean that particular characteristic of sight which attaches seeing to thinking, the eye to the mind. In architecture, vision refers to a particular category of perception linked to monocular perspectival vision. The monocular vision of the subject in architecture allows for all projections of space to be resolved on a single planimetric surface. It is therefore not surprising that perspective, with its ability to define and reproduce the perception of depth on a two-dimensional surface, should find architecture a waiting and wanting vehicle. Nor is it surprising that architecture soon began to conform itself to this monocular, rationalising vision – in its own body. Whatever the style, space was constituted as an understandable construct, organised around spatial elements such as axes, places, symmetries, etc. Perspective is even more virulent in architecture than in painting because of the imperious demands of the eye *and* the body to orient itself in architectural space through processes of rational perspectival ordering. It was thus not without cause that Brunelleschi's invention of one-point perspective should correspond to a time when there was a paradigm shift from the theological and theocentric to the anthropomorphic and anthropocentric views of the world. Perspective became the vehicle by which anthropocentric vision crystallised itself in the architecture that followed this shift.

Brunelleschi's projection system, however, was deeper in its effect than all subsequent stylistic changes because it confirmed vision as the dominant discourse in architecture from the 16th century to the present. Thus,

despite repeated changes in style from the Renaissance through Post-Modernism and despite many attempts to the contrary, the seeing human subject – monocular and anthropocentric – remains the primary discursive term of architecture.

The tradition of planimetric projection in architecture persisted unchallenged because it allowed the projection and hence the understanding of a three-dimensional space in two dimensions. In other disciplines – perhaps since Leibniz and certainly since Sartre – there has been a consistent attempt to demonstrate the problematic qualities inherent in vision but in architecture the sight/mind construct has persisted as the dominant discourse.

In an essay entitled 'Scopic Regimes of Modernity', Martin Jay notes that 'Baroque visual experience has a strongly tactile or haptic quality which prevents it from turning into the absolute ocular centrism of its Cartesian perspectivalist rival.' Norman Bryson, in his article 'The Gaze in the Expanded Field', introduces the idea of the gaze (*le regard*) as the looking back of the other. He discusses the gaze in terms of Sartre's intruder in *Being and Nothingness* or in terms of Lacan's concept of a darkness that cuts across the space of sight. Lacan also introduces the idea of a space looking back which he likens to a disturbance of the visual field of reason.

From time to time architecture has attempted to overcome its rationalising vision. If one takes for example the church of San Vitale in Ravenna one can explain the solitary column almost blocking the entry or the incomplete groin vaulting as an attempt to signal a change from a Pagan to a Christian architecture. Piranesi created similar effects with his architectural projections. Piranesi diffracted the monocular subject by creating perspectival visions with multiple vanishing points so that there was no way of correlating what was seen into a unified whole. Equally, Cubism attempted to deflect the relationship between a monocular subject and the object. The subject could no longer put the painting into some meaningful structure through the use of perspective. Cubism used a non-monocular perspectival condition: it flattened objects to the edges, it upturned objects, it undermined the stability of the picture plane. Architecture attempted similar dislocations through Constructivism and its own, albeit normalising, version of Cubism – the International Style. But this work only looked cubistic and modern, the subject remained rooted in a profound anthropocentric stability, comfortably upright and in place on a flat, tabular ground. There was no shift in the relationship between the subject and the object. While the object looked different it failed to displace the viewing subject. Though the buildings were sometimes conceptualised, by axonometric or isometric projection rather than by perspective, no consistent deflection of the subject was carried out. Yet Modernist sculpture did in many cases effect such a displacement of the subject. These dislocations were fundamental to Minimalism: the early work of Robert Morris, Michael Heizer and Robert Smithson. This historical project, however, was never taken up in architecture. The question now begs to be asked: why did architecture resist developments that were taking place in other disciplines? And further, why has the issue of vision never been

properly problematised in architecture?

It might be said that architecture never adequately thought through the problem of vision because it remained within the concept of the subject and the four walls. Architecture, unlike any other discipline, concretised vision. The hierarchy inherent in all architectural space begins as a structure for the mind's eye. It is perhaps the idea of interiority as a hierarchy between inside and outside that causes architecture to conceptualise itself ever more comfortably and conservatively in vision. The interiority of architecture more than any other discourse defined a hierarchy of vision articulated by inside and outside. The fact that one is actually both inside and outside with architecture, unlike painting or music, required vision to conceptualise itself in this way. As long as architecture refuses to take up the problem of vision, it will remain within a Renaissance or Classical view of its discourse.

Now what would it mean for architecture to take up the problem of vision? Vision can be defined as essentially a way of organising space and elements in space. It is a way of looking *at*, and defines a relationship between a subject and an object. Traditional architecture is structured so that any position occupied by a subject provides a means for understanding that position in relation to a particular spatial typology, such as a rotunda, a transept crossing, an axis, an entry. Any number of these typological conditionals deploy architecture as a screen for looking at.

The idea of a 'looking back' begins to displace the anthropocentric subject. Looking back does not require the object to become a subject, that is to anthropomorphise

the object. Looking back concerns the possibility of detaching the subject from the rationalisation of space. In other words to allow the subject to have a vision of space that no longer can be put together in the normalising, classicising or traditional construct of vision; an *other* space, where in fact the space 'looks back' at the subject. A possible first step in conceptualising this other space, would be to detach what one sees from what one knows – the eye from the mind. A second step would be to inscribe space in such a way as to endow it with the possibility of looking back at the subject. All architecture can be said to be already inscribed. Windows, doors, beams and columns are a kind of inscription. These make architecture known, they reinforce vision. Since no space is uninscribed, we do not see a window without relating it to an idea of window, this kind of inscription seems not only natural but also necessary to architecture. In order to have a looking back, it is necessary to rethink the idea of inscription. In the Baroque and Rococo such an inscription was in the plaster decoration that began to obscure the traditional form of functional inscription. This kind of 'decorative' description was thought too excessive when undefined by function. Architecture tends to resist this form of excess in a way which is unique amongst the arts, precisely because of the power and pervasive nature of functional inscription. The anomalous column at San Vitale inscribes space in a way that was at the time foreign to the eye. This is also true of the columns in the staircase at the Wexner Center however most of such inscriptions are the result of design intention, the will of an authorial subjective expression which then only

reconstitutes vision as before. To dislocate vision might require an inscription which is the result of an outside text which is neither overly determined by design expression or function. But how could such an inscription of an outside text translate into space?

Suppose for a moment that architecture could be conceptualised as a Moebius strip, with an unbroken continuity between interior and exterior. What would this mean for vision? Gilles Deleuze has proposed just such a possible continuity with his idea of the fold. For Deleuze, folded space articulates a new relationship between vertical and horizontal, figure and ground, inside and out – all structures articulated by traditional vision. Unlike the space of classical vision, the idea of folded space denies framing in favour of a temporal modulation. The fold no longer privileges planimetric projection; instead there is a variable curvature. Deleuze's idea of folding is more radical than origami, because it contains no narrative, linear sequence; rather, in terms of traditional vision it contains a quality of the unseen.

Folding changes the traditional space of vision. That is, it can be considered to be *e*ffective; it functions, it shelters, it is meaningful, it frames, it is aesthetic. Folding also constitutes a move from *e*ffective to *a*ffective space. Folding is not another subject expressionism, a promiscuity, but rather unfolds in space alongside of its functioning and its meaning in space – it has what might be called an excessive condition or affect. Folding is a type of affective space which concerns those aspects that are not associated with the *a*ffective, that are more than reason, meaning and function.

In order to change the

relationship of perspectival projection to three-dimensional space it is necessary to change the relationship between project drawing and real space. This would mean that one would no longer be able to draw with any level of meaningfulness the space that is being projected. For example, when it is no longer possible to draw a line that stands for some scale relationship to another line in space, it has nothing to do with reason, of the connection of the mind to the eye. The deflection from that line in space means that there no longer exists a one-to-one scale correspondence.

My folded projects are a primitive beginning. In them the subject understands that he or she can no longer conceptualise experience in space in the same way that he or she did in the gridded space. They attempt to provide this dislocation of the subject from effective space; an idea of presentness. Once the environment becomes affective, inscribed with another logic or an ur-logic, one which is no longer translatable into the vision of the mind, then reason becomes detached from vision. While we can still understand space in terms of its function, structure and aesthetic – we are still within the 'four walls' – somehow reason becomes detached from the affective condition of the environment itself. This begins to produce an environment that 'looks back' – that is, the environment seems to have an order that we can perceive even though it does not seem to mean anything. It does not seek to be understood in the traditional way of architecture yet it possess some sense of 'aura', an ur-logic which is the sense of something outside of our vision. Yet one that is not another subjective expression. Folding is only one of perhaps

many strategies for dislocating vision – dislocating the hierarchy of interior and exterior that pre-empts vision.

The Alteka Tower project begins simultaneously with an 'el' shape drawn in both plan and section. Here, a change in the relationship of perspectival projection to three-dimensional space changes the relationship between project drawing and real space. In this sense, these drawings would have little relationship to the space that is being projected. For example it is no longer possible to draw a line that stands for some scale relationship to another line in the space of the project, thus the drawn lines no longer have anything to do with reason, the connection of the mind to the eye. The drawn lines are folded with some ur-logic according to sections of a fold in René Thom's catastrophe theory. These folded plans and sections in turn create an object, which is cut into from the ground floor to the top.

When the environment is inscribed or folded in such a way the individual no longer remains the discursive function; the individual is no longer required to understand or interpret space. Questions such as what the space means are no longer relevant. It is not just that the environment is detached from vision, but that it also presents its own vision, a vision that looks back at the individual. The inscription is no longer concerned with aesthetics or with meaning but with some other order. It is only necessary to perceive the fact that this other order exists; this perception alone dislocates the knowing subject.

The fold presents the possibility of an alternative to the gridded space of the Cartesian order. The fold produces a dislocation of the dialectical distinction between

figure and ground; in the process it animates what Gilles Deleuze calls a smooth space. Smooth space presents the possibility of overcoming or exceeding the grid. The grid remains in place and the four walls will always exist but they are in fact overtaken by the folding of space. Here there is no longer one planimetric view which is then extruded to provide a sectional space. Instead it is no longer possible to relate a vision of space in a two-dimensional drawing to the three-dimensional reality of a folded space. Drawing no longer has any scale value relationship to the three-dimensional environment. This dislocation of the two-dimensional drawing from the three-dimensional reality also begins to dislocate vision, inscribed by this ur-logic. There are no longer grid datum planes for the upright individual.

Alteka is not merely a surface architecture or a surface folding. Rather, the folds create an affective space, a dimension in the space that dislocates the discursive function of the human subject and thus vision, and at the same moment creates a condition of time, of an event in which there is the possibility of the environment looking back at the subject, the possibility of the *gaze*.

The gaze according to Maurice Blanchot is that possibility of seeing which remains covered up by vision. The gaze opens the possibility of seeing what Blanchot calls the light lying within darkness. It is not the light of the dialectic of light/dark, but it is the light of an otherness, which lies hidden within presence. It is the capacity to see this otherness which is repressed by vision. The looking back, the gaze, exposes architecture to another light, one which could not have been seen before.

Architecture will continue to stand up, to deal with gravity, to have 'four walls'. But these four walls no longer need to be expressive of the mechanical paradigm. Rather they could deal with the possibility of these other discourses, the other affective senses of sound, touch and of that light lying within the darkness.

Alteka Tower, Tokyo; and previous page: Banyoles Olympic Hotel, Barcelona

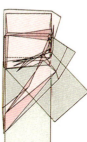

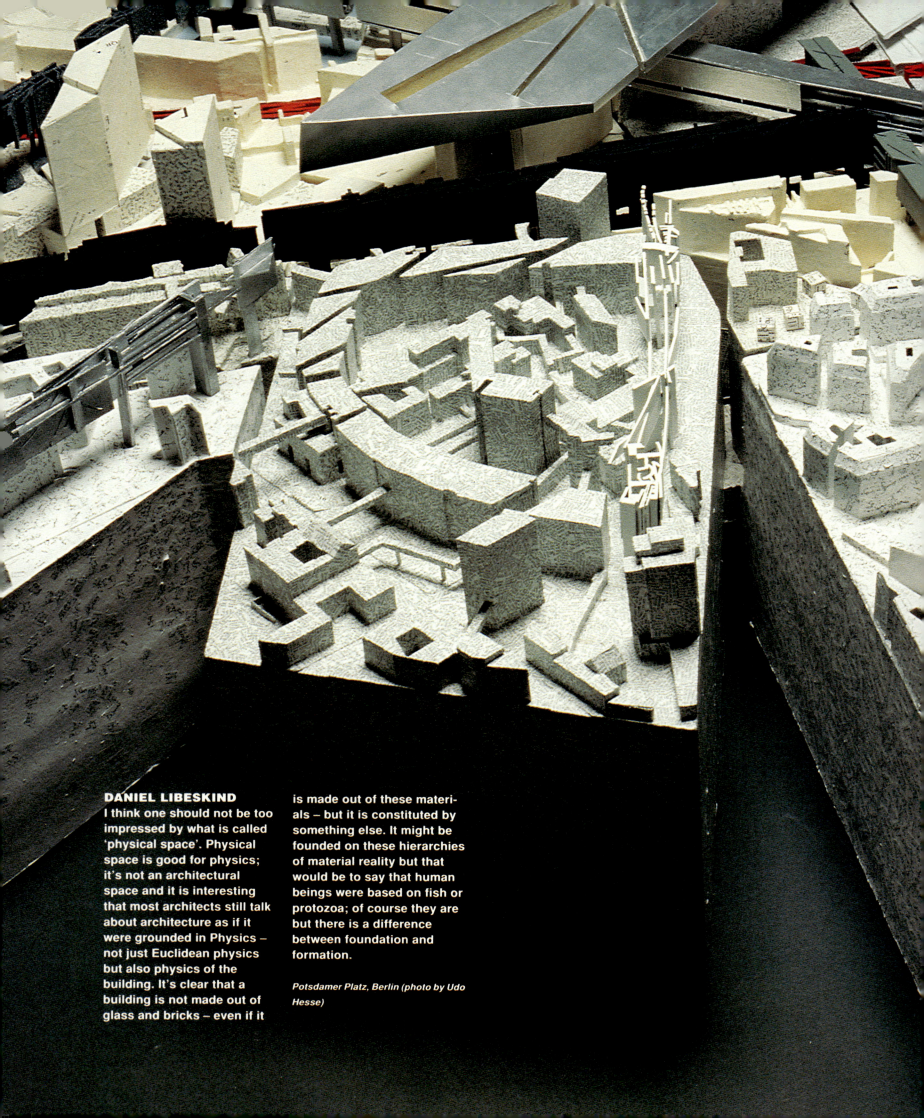

DANIEL LIBESKIND
I think one should not be too impressed by what is called 'physical space'. Physical space is good for physics; it's not an architectural space and it is interesting that most architects still talk about architecture as if it were grounded in Physics – not just Euclidean physics but also physics of the building. It's clear that a building is not made out of glass and bricks – even if it is made out of these materials – but it is constituted by something else. It might be founded on these hierarchies of material reality but that would be to say that human beings were based on fish or protozoa; of course they are but there is a difference between foundation and formation.

Potsdamer Platz, Berlin (photo by Udo Hesse)

WILL ALSOP
'I belong to a generation of architects that gets very anxious about self expression . . . But I see architecture as a form of artistic activity, and I'm not embarrassed about it.'

If Alsop's design looks futuristic it is because he is at heart an artist. His first ideas for a building do not take the form of sketches or models, but are seemingly abstract compositions where he experiments with form and colour.

Hamburg Ferry Terminal

PETER WILSON
England, and to a large extent America, are today's architectural backwaters; it is only there that the question 'Does a new Modernism exist' is asked. Elsewhere, 'The Second Modernism' is well underway. It is not a revival or play with forms of 'Heroic Modernism'. It is architecture consequent to today's technological and perceptual revolution, an architecture of clear unmannered forms which accept and give measure to the discontinuous post-industrial field.

Folly, Osaka (photo by Kobayashi)

ODILE DECQ
Are not the new systems of relationship between space and its limits apparent when the entire facade of a building is a single suspended film of glass with wind bracing provided by a structure set two metres in front of it? In such a case, the physical and visual limits of space are totally dissociated.

'La Tour sans fin', Paris (photo by Georges Fessy)

MARK FISHER
Popular culture is ephemeral, but most architecture is designed to be permanent. The high-brow dredging of popular culture to make Pop Art is OK for paintings. They can be hidden when they go out of fashion, and then rehung from time to time as historical curiosities. For architecture the only escape from old fashion is demolition. Long-life buildings are anathema to Pop architecture.

Rolling Stones 'Steel Wheels' stage set

ITSUKO HASEGAWA
A Search for New Concepts through Filtering my Life in Tokyo

Land possesses certain dormant qualities in the same way that a human body retains memories of its origins somewhere within it. My objective is to extract those dormant qualities and to make them manifest architecturally, I call this approach 'Architecture a Second Nature'. In other words, to create architecture is to use a completely different vocabulary in expressing what has been experienced iby a human being. So my architecture is created through a process of filtering the spirit of my own life in Tokyo. The theme of my lecture today is a search for new concepts through filtering the spirit of my life in Tokyo.

The Urban Scene of Tokyo
Tokyo is a city which expanded by embodying versatile factors and accumulating invisible systems without applying urban development planning. It continues to transfigure with no composition or coherence. It has no place to go but becomes saturated and, therefore, a site of extraordinary dynamism. It has already exceeded the boundary of a modern city and is assuming a serious aspect of an ultra modern city. While it retains an Asiatic village style in its total space or people or objects, huge economic structures and high technology permeate throughout, making it a swollen, chaotic city. However, from an Asian point of view, and looking at it historically since the Edo period, the sensual artistic traditions of the Edo culture seem to remain in its space and in people's consciousness. Various disciplines, solidarity, and net-

works have made the city safe, while amenities such as residential sunshine and ventilation, based on the Japanese concept of nature, are legally protected. Now that people are affluent, they are seeking spiritual fulfilment and a better environment. I regard the present chaotic situation as the precursor to a new, higher dimensional space which will open up, rather than a catastrophe to follow. We should face chaos without fear.

As Freud said, 'we can produce a new and fresh era, after overcoming the strange unknown and darkness lying ahead of us.' We should look forward to reaching beauty and freedom beyond the present obstacles. The city planners, unable to stand the expansion of urban space far beyond their expectation, as cities grew into increasingly complex and gigantic communities at an enormous speed, gave up and changed their venue to small town planning in depopulated areas.

Those able to bring new order and freedom to Tokyo are no longer the city planners. They may well be film directors or musicians or mathematicians or scientists, as in the suggested Reflex Image of Wim Wenders.

Scenes Presented by Architecture
The bird's eye view of Tokyo is a forest of large and small buildings. Close-up, each building is full of ultra-modern and unique expression and detail. It is said that architecture is partly a direct expression of absolute commercial greed. Tokyo is the theatre where symbols of the consumer society flit. Super-technology covers the entire Tokyo urban area, turniing everything into a kind of media, where the real and unreal can hardly be told apart,

while the architectural profile vanishes. In the electronic information society where invisible signals flow, architecture is a component of an intelligent and emotional city, where nature and technology coexist naturally. Traditional Japanese architecture looks dignified, but, in fact, is a living space and conception based on free and vague rules of Nature, without being tied to architectural precision and strict spatial concepts, as with houses described in Kamo no Choumei's 'Houjouki', and 'Tsurezuregusa' by the monk Kenko Hoshi. This may relate to the present situation.

Architecture looks like a mere component of a city. Even if it were a mere component, it may give new experience to people and trigger their joy by stimulating their emotions or consciousness. Positive and dynamic new architecture may be developed to rescue cities from catastrophe with versatile and comprehensive functions which can be generated through a power imbalance. Or the city may be constructed by an assembly of individually well-designed architecture. As architecture is a live experiencing space, an overall criticism such as 'image' or 'literature' may be difficult. As the change in people's consciousness speeds up, it is also time for architecture to reinforce it. The absence of architectural critics should be a serious problem. Today is a time where architectural criticism is badly needed.

The Technological Scene
It was always the on-site worker who felt the futility and disillusion of the industry-centred society and sensed the direction of post-industrial society in Japan, and never the academics. These are common citizens who participate in traditional festivals each season held ever since Japan

was an agricultural country.

They write classical Japanese poems such as Haiku and Senryu, and engage in cultural activities such as traditional shows; they are people who are good with their hands. Our citizen's society is symbolised by cartoons such as 'Tetsuwan (Iron Arm) Atom' about a boy with iron arms, with factories full of robots. In Kumamoto Prefecture, the 'Kumamoto Artpolis Programme' is being implemented, which intends to design all public buildings in the Prefecture by domestic and foreign architects.

Now, citizens are raising loud objections to architects' proposals to build public condominiums. They are striving to restore architecture back to the hands of the users. People are moving to protect their life and environment at the grassroots level, and there are now professional town planners who rose from these citizens. Being an informed society attracting all the people and commodities, unipolar concentration is accelerating in Tokyo. Sprung from technology, greed and dreams amplify, causing a dynamic reality which even absorbs art into public manners and customs. Science and technology have entered the human electronics age combining living creatures and machines on common grounds, replacing the old-fashioned mode of the 20th century where nature and men conflict.

Molecular biology discovered that every living creature has DNA genes. Subsequently, life has been comprehended as a complete and informed micro-system, which opened its utilities on energy-saving type technology. Thus, men and nature, science and technology can stand on common ground and interrelate whilst maintaining their own unique features.

They are developing into a life-sized, life-caring discipline even reaching out to the sensual domain, which may wake up the mysterious subconscious of people, and in that sense what could also be called a feminine and deeper thinking, and a new world involving religion and science altogether. Now, as we enter the age of total systems, new types of architects like Sherman are needed by society.

Architectural Scenes as a Second Nature

Construction of a new structure should mean replacing the topography and space lost by a construction with an even richer nature generated by the old one. The new architecture should be a mound to bury the inevitably destroyed nature by the construction, and an opportunity to resume communication with Nature.

I have brought up the long historical theme of 'Nature' embodied in my theory of 'Architecture as a Second Nature', which answers the contemporary spirit. This means a departure from the concept that architecture is a product of reason. It should be a substance entirely separate from other matters. Indeed, architecture should generate a place for people to live as a part of nature which lies in human consciousness; nature should include total human life, which is accommodated in the common ecology.

Another way to look at it is to recover the emotional side of culture, which has been cut off from the rich yet materialistic world in the name of rationality of modern society, allowing no room for human mutual sympathy, or to open our ears to listen to the mysterious music of the universe. This means to aim and build a new type of architecture under the leadership of the citizen's society on the basis of modern science and technology, where rationality and irrationality, internationality and locality can live together in Nature.

People are beginning to notice the appearance of the 'Second Nature', as the construction of a new environment by Tokyo's technology makes progress. I have persisted in an *ad hoc* style of development, rather than an attitude of exclusive development . This means an inclusive type of architecture which accepts various factors in a comprehensive plan. I believe architecture can stand on a popular rationale embracing a multipolar value system, rather than a logical rationality based on unipolar value. Such a stance will give rise in people's subconscious to a consensus, and trigger a feminist paradigm. To remain in Tokyo to continue my theme of creating 'Architecture as a Second Nature' by which I mean the latent relationship between human beings and the environment, is something I intend to do for some while.

STM House, Tokyo

suppress them? As we, Coop Himmelblau, are Viennese, we have a close connection to Freud who taught us that suppression requires a tremendous amount of energy. We would like to spend this energy on our projects.

The safe and sound world of architecture no longer exists. It will never exist again. 'Open Architecture' means consciousness and an open mind.

Melrose I (photo by Tom Bonner)

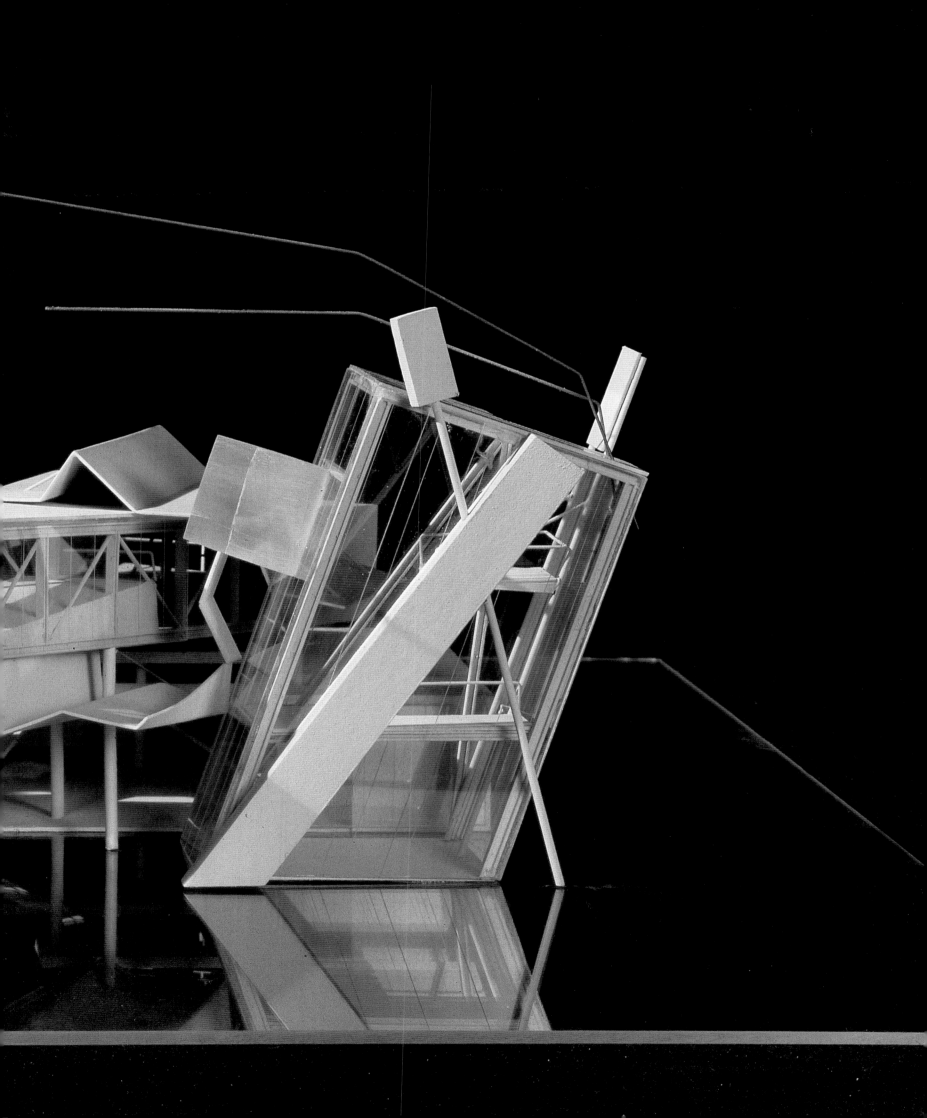

THOM MAYNE
Architecture is a form of communication. It aims to reach and affect the emotional life of its viewer. What is important is that the language remains conceptual and open in nature, that it does not replace investigation and that it assimilates and resonates the specific aspects of its environment. It is the ability to absorb the idiosyncratic which, in the end, gives the work its energy, immediacy and life.

8201 Beverly Boulevard, Los Angeles (photo by Tom Bonner)

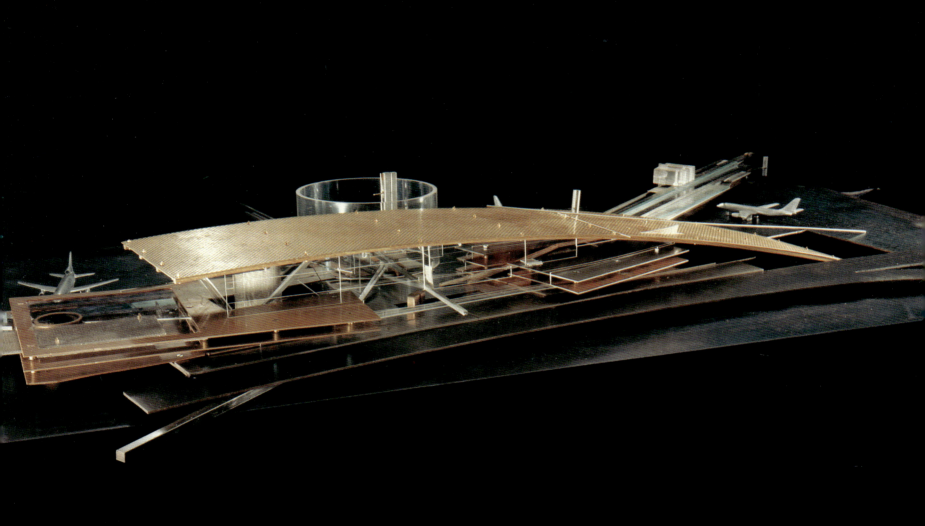

PETER PRAN
The overall design has as its main statement and strength a long, curved, floating steel roof that seems to come out of the ground. This elegantly and delicately detailed steel roof expresses a poetic statement of movement and flight. The design creates a feeling of anticipation and delight in the passengers; it celebrates the many aspects of flying.

JFK Airport, New York (photo by Dan Cornish)

BERNARD TSCHUMI
Architecture is not about the conditions of design, but about the design of conditions. Our object today is not to fulfil the conditions of construction, but to achieve the construction of conditions that will dislocate the most traditional and regressive aspects of our society and simultaneously reorganise these elements in the most liberating way, where our experience becomes the experience of events organised and strategised through architecture. Strategy is a key word today in architecture. No more masterplans, no more locating in a fixed place, but a new heterotopia that is what our cities are striving towards, and here we architects must help them by intensifying the rich collision of events and spaces.

'Le Fresnoy', Tourcoing, France
(photo by Dan Cornish)

LEBBEUS WOODS
Architecture embraces and subsumes physics as well as the other forms of the invention of knowledge. Thus architecture is the principal experimental laboratory for human beings. Even when it attempts to mimic the past (Historicism), or to control the future (Functionalism), architecture yields for its makers and inhabitants a rich tableau of experimental data, ever changing, highly personal and unique, always only of the present existential moment.

Berlin Free Zone

STUDIO ASYMPTOTE

A microchip of infinitesimal dimension has been devised that will alter the commodity of history. Imagine if you will, a memory exchange containing all of history, all information and all means of knowing. In such a place one could barter and trade thought, diminishing certain stocks while increasing the value of others.

Steel Cloud, West Coast Gateway, Los Angeles

GÜNTHER ZAMP KELP

The annihilation of the obje which one finds in the abstract concepts of mode art becomes reality in the actual social space by virtu of media projection . . . Architecture has to change As a link between reality ar projection of the media it remains true to its nature — creating space for the organisation of society. At the same time it will have to take into account the fact that its image together with social events have to play a important role in the projec tive part of our world. *Heinrich Klotz*

House behind River Scenery, Meerbusch

MICHAEL ROTONDI

Is it possible to document our discoveries, to describe what we see and feel – our intuition – in the things that we make?

There is only one way to test this idea and that is to construct it again and again.

CDLT 1, 2 (photo by Benny Chan)

ERIC OWEN MOSS

At some level, every project involves a kind of manipulation or transformation of what's given, either literally or figuratively or both. What I don't want to do, is give you back something that is monochromatic, (somehow single-minded and simple-minded are close to each other) so that if something is simply symmetrical, or simply balanced, or simply linear, or simply a narrative, it's simple-minded. That is not my experience of the world.

Samitaur Offices, Los Angeles

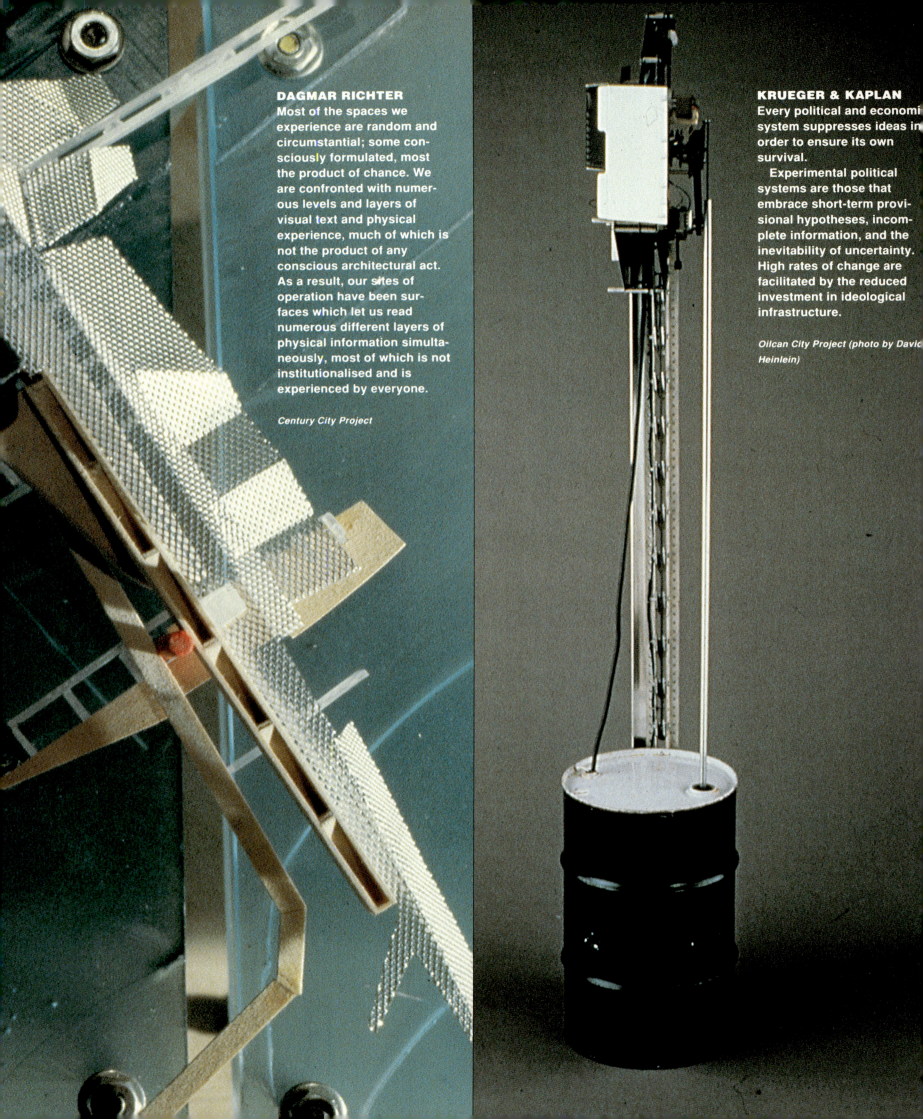

DAGMAR RICHTER
Most of the spaces we
experience are random and
circumstantial; some con-
sciously formulated, most
the product of chance. We
are confronted with numerous levels and layers of
visual text and physical
experience, much of which is
not the product of any
conscious architectural act.
As a result, our sites of
operation have been sur-
faces which let us read
numerous different layers of
physical information simultaneously, most of which is not
institutionalised and is
experienced by everyone.

Century City Project

KRUEGER & KAPLAN
Every political and economi
system suppresses ideas in
order to ensure its own
survival.
    Experimental political
systems are those that
embrace short-term provi-
sional hypotheses, incom-
plete information, and the
inevitability of uncertainty.
High rates of change are
facilitated by the reduced
investment in ideological
infrastructure.

*Oilcan City Project (photo by David
Heinlein)*

JAPANESE ARCHITECTURE II

SHIN TAKAMATSU, SOLARIS BUILDING, AMAGASAKI, HYOGO

Architectural Design
Edited by Andreas C Papadakis

JAPANESE ARCHITECTURE II

ABOVE: MINORU TAKEYAMA, TOKYO INTERNATIONAL PORT TERMINAL
OPPOSITE: ARATA ISOZAKI, ART TOWER, MITO

ACADEMY EDITIONS • LONDON

Acknowledgements

by Guest Editor Botond Bognar

In preparing this issue, I was greatly helped by a large number of people whose contribution I would like to acknowledge hereby with great appreciation. These contributions include, first of all, the architects themselves who provided graphic and textual material relevant to their works featured; Toyo Ito and Professor Vladimir Krstic wrote excellent pieces that broaden greatly the argument forwarded here, and I am grateful for their skill and dedication. I would like to thank R Alan Forrester, the Director of the School of Architecture at the University of Illinois, for his continuing support of my work; moreover, the preparation of this issue would not have been possible without the kind assistance of the staff of the School, especially Tracy Hawkins and Jane Cook who typed the manuscript over and over. Thank you indeed! Some of the photographic material was generously provided by the following photographers: Yasuhiro Ishimoto, Shigeru Anzai, Tadao Ando, Mitsuo Matsuoka, Tomio Ohashi, Itsuko Hasegawa, and Vladimir Krstic. Also, I would like to express my gratitude to my friends for their invaluable help and assistance while I collected the material in Japan; they include: Tadao and Yumiko Ando, Hajime Yatsuka, Minoru Takeyama, Ryoji and Hideko Suzuki, Professor Koji Yagi, Toyo Ito, Itsuko Hasegawa, Takefumi Aida, Hiromi Fujii, Atsushi Kitagawara, Shin Takamatsu, Yasumitsu Matsunaga and last but not least, Nariaki Suzuki, our dear Dozo-bachi.

Photographic Credits
All photographs are by Botond Bognar with the exception of the following:
Yashiro Ishimoto p2, 28-31; Vladimir Krstic pp24-27; Tomio Ohashi pp38, 40; Mitsuo Matsuoka pp52;
courtesy of Tadao Ando p53, 56-57; Koji Horiuchi p58; courtesy of Itsuko Hasegawa p60; Shigeo Ogawa p82

EDITOR
Dr Andreas C Papadakis

CONSULTANTS: Catherine Cooke, Terry Farrell, Kenneth Frampton, Charles Jencks
Heinrich Klotz, Leon Krier, Robert Maxwell, Demetri Porphyrios, Kenneth Powell, Colin Rowe, Derek Walker
EDITORIAL TEAM: Maggie Toy (House Editor), Vivian Constantinopoulos, Helen Castle
DESIGN TEAM: Andrea Bettella (Senior Designer), Mario Bettella, Owen Thomas
SUBSCRIPTIONS MANAGER: Mira Joka BUSINESS MANAGER: Sheila de Vallée

First published in Great Britain in 1992 by *Architectural Design* an imprint of the
ACADEMY GROUP LTD, 42 LEINSTER GARDENS, LONDON W2 3AN
ISBN: 1-85490-132-X (UK)

The Publishers and Editor do not hold themselves responsible for the opinions expressed by the
writers of articles or letters in this magazine
Copyright of articles and illustrations may belong to individual writers or artists
Architectural Design Profile 99 is published as part of *Architectural Design* Vol 62 9-10 /1992
Architectural Design Magazine is published six times a year and is available by subscription

Published in the United States of America by
ST MARTIN'S PRESS, 175 FIFTH AVENUE, NEW YORK, NY 10010
ISBN: 0-312-08109-X (USA)

Printed and bound in Singapore

Contents

KISHO KUROKAWA, OKINAWA PREFECTURAL GOVERNMENT HEADQUARTERS, NAHA

ARCHITECTURAL DESIGN PROFILE No 99

JAPANESE ARCHITECTURE II
GUEST-EDITED BY BOTOND BOGNAR

TRADITION AND THE NEW IN JAPANESE ARCHITECTURE

While Western architects and critics agonise over the rise and fall of stylistic fashions, and 'tradition' is invoked as an anchor amid the storms of change, Japan eagerly embraces the late 20th century and forges an architecture of transition which is the frank expression of a technological, consumerist society. Japanese architecture has come of age. It no longer repels or frightens (as the mechanistic visions of the Metabolist school perhaps did): it is inviting, fascinating, diverse, free in spirit, responsive to nature, and rich in emotion.

The wonder is that Japan's pre-eminent position in the realm of creative architecture is only grudgingly conceded in Europe and North America. Only now are Japanese architects building on any scale in the West – Isozaki, for example, in Florida and Barcelona, Maki in California and Ando at Seville – and they are generally established designers born between the mid 20s and the Second World War. The younger generation has yet to make its mark internationally, in terms of completed buildings. (Three of the leaders of the middle generation, the professional stars of the 1990s, were born in the fateful year of 1941: Ando, Hasegawa and Ito.) But can this situation continue much longer, given the reservoir of talent in Japan?

There is every reason to believe that Japan may soon be the critical influence in the development of world architecture. There are, perhaps, good reasons why the new Japanese architecture cannot easily be assimilated abroad. The most obvious explanation is that it represents a specific response to Japanese society. The current economic crisis in Japan – a breathing space after years of unrestrained growth – only underlines the basic strengths of the country's economy. For more than 30 years, Japan has boomed, producing the most phenomenal consumer society in modern history. If the North American model of society mesmerised the Japanese in the immediate postwar years, they have since created an economic, social and cultural order of equivalent potency.

The rate of change in Japanese society continues to amaze Westerners. Staggering land values – especially in Tokyo – make frequent redevelopment a practical necessity, as buildings cease to meet changing needs. In Japan, the age of the ephemeral building has dawned. The role of the architect in this process is uncertain: mass-produced, off-the-peg buildings, customised to suit the requirements of users, are a practical option. Yet ephemerality also stimulates invention and freedom and a shift away from the monumentalism of the recent past.

Tange (b 1913) and Isozaki (b 1931) are the pillars of modern Japanese architecture – even if Tange is now – inevitably – a sad shadow and Isozaki is occasionally sensational to the point of vulgarity. They stand at the head of a school of monumentalism which certainly includes the work of Takamatsu, Hara, and Shinohara. The adjective 'monumentalist' could less obviously be applied to that of Tadao Ando, who is probably the most fashionable Japanese architect on the current international scene. Ando's buildings, notable amongst them the famous series of churches, have an evocative, enigmatic, surreal quality which suggests spiritual depth. For the Westerner, Ando's work seems to embody typically Japanese values in its allusive use of traditional metaphors yet it stands apart from the most fertile stream of architectural development in contemporary Japan.

The 'runaway architectural culture' of Japan (as Botond Bognar describes it) accepts and even celebrates this phenomenon, using it as the basis for an architecture of change and impermanence. Toyo Ito, Itsuko Hasegawa, Hiromi Fujii, and Kiko Mozuna, amongst others, have questioned the old axioms about architecture in the context of time. (Ito looks forward to buildings which 'appear for an event and disappear when the event ends'.) It is tempting to link this tendency with the realities of the Japanese development scene – where a building can actually be demolished within a few years, possibly without ever having been occupied. Yet there is a deeper meaning, a reference back to a 'floating world' of fashion, which cloaks deeper truths, and an implied critique of the consumer society. In this light, considerations of 'style' become refreshingly irrelevant: a whole new way of critical thinking is a prerequisite to an understanding of Japanese architecture today.

It is no accident that some of the most memorable of recent Japanese buildings are located not in cities but in locations of great natural beauty: Ando's churches being prime examples. Hasegawa has stated her wish to make architecture 'responsive to the ecosystem, as all of human existence is ultimately encompassed by nature'. Hiroshi Hara's Iida Museum, set amidst mountain scenery, evokes the quiet of a forest. Impermanence is the essence of Japan today. But the new architecture of Japan looks beyond contemporary society towards a new way of designing which is in tune with the natural world and with the essence of humanity. Its obsession with the ephemeral is not just a corollary of the electronic society. It represents a vision of man and nature which is surely a central theme in the new global architecture of the *fin de siècle*. Defying mere imitation, the new Japanese architecture invites us to redefine the relationship between the world of nature and the world as created by mankind: which should be the central concern for humanity at the end of the 20th century. Japan offers a view of the architecture of the future: *now*.

ACP/KP   *Itsuko Hasegawa, Nagoya Pavilion*

7

BOTOND BOGNAR

BETWEEN REALITY AND FICTION
Japanese Architecture in the 1990s or the New Fin de Siècle

So many diverse meanings are established beneath the surface of the image that it presents only an enigmatic face. And its power is no longer to teach but to fascinate . . . Freed from wisdom and from the teaching that organised it, the image begins to gravitate about its own madness.

Paradoxically, this liberation derives from a proliferation of meaning, from a self-multiplication of significance, weaving relationships so numerous, so intertwined, so rich, that they can no longer be deciphered except in the esoterism of knowledge. Things themselves become so burdened with attributes, signs, allusions that they finally lose their own form. Meaning is no longer read in an immediate perception, the figure no longer speaks for itself; between the knowledge which animates it and the form into which it is transposed, a gap widens. It is free for the dream.

Michel Foucault, *Madness and Civilisation – A History of Insanity in the Age of Reason*[1]

From an Accelerated Environment to a Post-Urban Society

The volume and quality of architectural production in Japan have long fascinated and/or puzzled all those who regularly, and more so occasionally, followed up the developments of this architecture in the past several decades. The 1990s are no exception; in fact recent events seem to reinforce such experiences in the extreme. Building activity is more extensive than ever, while the variety of design encompasses a spectrum previously unimaginable. Yet the most striking phenomenon today is the speed with which the built environment, that is the city, is changing and in which vicissitude architecture now finds itself caught up almost inescapably.

This is, of course, not to say that Japan was not formerly a dynamic nation. On the contrary. Ever since the country opened its gates to the rest of the world in the middle of the 19th century, Japanese progress and the pace of change have never been anything less than rapid. The 'Japanese miracle' in the 1960s, the continued economic boom thereafter, and the more recent evolution of a highly-advanced consumer-cum-information society, along with other factors, have had a profound, explosive impact on the whole country, first of all on the course, extensiveness and unique form of its urbanisation. Foreigners visiting Japan from time to time have commented on the difficulties they had in recognising certain urban areas and even larger districts in metropolitan regions such as Osaka, Nagoya, Hiroshima, and most of all Tokyo, upon returning there after only a few years.

By now, however, such changes have reached hitherto unheard-of proportions and so, one cannot go to Japan frequently enough without experiencing some dramatic transformations. Most noticeable was up until now new constructions took place on previously empty lots or replaced old shacks, inferior structures or dilapidated blocks; today, however, many new projects are built by way of demolishing existing buildings that had been completed just a few decades ago, or as recently as a few years ago and were, in all fairness, still in excellent condition. Moreover, examples of razed buildings include such prominent representatives of Japan's post-war architecture as Kenzo Tange's Tokyo City Hall of 1957 or Itsuko Hasegawa's Bizan Hall of 1984 in Shizuoka City. The first, upon the completion of Tange's own new, and highly controversial, City Hall in the Shinjuku district, has given way to Raphael Vinoly's Tokyo International Forum, now under construction for completion in 1955, while the latter, after being partially demolished, then extended, has been altered beyond recognition.

Yet the line does not stop here. Masaharu Takasaki's Crystal Light Building, a company guest house complex of 1987 in Tokyo, has been pulled down in 1990 without ever being used at all. It has since been replaced by another, more profitable structure. Among other well-known recent projects, but already earmarked for removal, we find for example Hajime Yatsuka's Tarlazzi Building of 1987 as well. In a situation like this, as Toyo Ito once commented, many architects expect their projects to last only a few years. To prove this point, Ito's own Nomad Restaurant in Tokyo's glitzy Roppongi area had been commissioned outright for a mere couple of years' use; designed within two weeks in 1986, it has already been replaced with something else.[2]

With the increase of such practices, one may appropriately ask the question: just what exactly is going on in Japanese cities today? The answer obviously is complex, yet, to single out one major force behind these developments, it is the progress of Japanese consumerism 'in overdrive', along with one of its phenomena, the sky-rocketing land prices. No doubt land has always been scarce and expensive in Japan, but with the new economic prosperity and affluence, this is even more so. New investments and construction in any urban area push up the value of real estate in the whole vicinity and this rapid upward spiralling move is often boasted by speculators' urge for fast and extra large profit.

Statistical data reveal that, for example in the Ginza district of central Tokyo in 1987, one square foot of land could go for as much as US$ 28,000.[3] It goes without say-

Kenzo Tange, City Hall, Tokyo

Masaharu Takasaki, Crystal Light Guest house, Tokyo

Shibuya Station Square, Tokyo

Yatsuka Hajime, Tarlazzi Building, Tokyo

Shibuya Station Square, Tokyo

ing that the amount of tax to be paid after such land is equally high. Therefore, to profit from the property, landowners are prompted to invest in construction as soon as possible, and then to rent the available space to high-powered businesses, fashion retail, media, advertising, etc. And, although construction cost in general is higher in Japan than in the US, relative to the land price, it is still only a small portion of the total investment. Thus, as Yutaka Hikosaka notes, 'buildings forming the cityscape are [often merely] pawns in the land-management game. Today land, which represents the biggest rights and interests, is the central item of the economy, [and] used as a capitalist prop for politics of a non-ideological nature.'[4] In the fiercely competitive environment, profitability demands the continued attention and/or attraction of both the public and media, and so newness, novelty and imageability are often primary criteria in commissioning new edifices. Hence architecture and urbanism tend, in an increasing fashion, towards the quality of changeable signs and often advertising, whose strategy of fascination with images is to elicit and exploit human desires. The ultimate purpose is to turn people into *consumers* who are then irresistibly attracted to their world as *commodity* .

On the other hand, the Japanese city, represented best by Tokyo, displays unique characteristics which, inherited from the past, contribute to and hasten significantly these developments. Chaotic conditions, congestion, radical heterogeneity, the variety and proliferation of signs, along with the lack of any sensible centre or regulating order are well-known features of capricious Japanese urbanism. Nevertheless, there is another, less obvious, but equally important aspect that articulates urban life in Japan.

Japanese homes are not only cramped together but are also extremely small and, except for a relative minority, can hardly be used for much more than a place to retire for the night.[5] As such, they are usually not places for entertaining guests or meeting others. These activities have to and do take place overwhelmingly outside the home, in the city: on the streets or other public places like the innumerable smaller or larger pubs, bars, cafés, tea parlours, clubs, shopping arcades, etc, not to mention one's own office that most employees regard as their larger home or family. Moreover, people routinely commute several hours daily between their homes and places of work or between places of interest. Consequently, Japanese cities, metropolitan areas, and the urban life within, have acquired apparently paradoxical dimensions and can be interpreted in two different ways. First, the urban realm now functions as a kind of large common living room of the citizens, whereby the city often appears as having *no exterior*. Second, this city, being always on the move, bustling, and restless, has problematised or relativised the traditional notions of permanent residence and home whereby it can be considered, in Toyo Ito's words, as a 'continuously' temporary camp of 'urban nomads'.[6] This of course also raises the issue of another kind of 'homelessness' in the Japanese city, in conjunction with the problem of the *lost interior*.

Thus compounded with the special attributes of the historically evolved Japanese architecture and urbanism, with the traditional predisposition of the Japanese towards

a 'floating world', as well as with the overall penetration of the most advanced information and media technologies into contemporary life, recent late-capitalist society in Japan has produced and is riding on an *accelerated environment*, that is 'cities on the fast lane'. More than merely an ephemeral realm, this is a radically volatile world with a 'ruined map', wherein a sense of reality is profoundly undermined by the insidious forces of simulation or, conversely, wherein reality is now rendered as a dream-like fiction. If Disneyworld could be called 'the ultimate mediated environment, . . . a particular extreme of non-reality', then Tokyo comes very close to this world indeed.[7] And, in so doing, Tokyo is also incomparably more delirious than New York, about which Rem Koolhaas wrote so incisively a few years ago.[8]

It may be said that for the first time in the history of architecture, we have reached a stage of urbanism wherein the essence of the built environment is produced as, and/or by, images and information. That is to say, the city is rendered largely as media; and in this sense we may talk about, as Koji Taki has pointed out, the emergence of the first 'post-urban society' in Japan.[9]

Large-Scale Projects and the Process of Globalisation

All these developments have had, and continue to have, other profound consequences on the quality and nature of contemporary architectural production. The consequences, however, are not necessarily unequivocally negative. On the one hand we unquestionably find the appalling and overall signs of trivialisation and commercialisation, and the eclipse of a critical self-awareness along with the weakening, if not complete disappearance of the public realm in the city. On the other hand, and not without some inherent paradox, there is an increased architectural activity and a growing popular interest in design as well as in the urban environment. Tokyo and other large metropolises in Japan appear as being continuously 'under construction', there is hardly any place in the city where there would not be some kind of feverish building activity going on, often on a large scale. The signs of a building boom have been apparent for quite some time and continue to manifest vitality in this respect despite a somewhat slower economy.[10]

Designers running small atelier-type architectural offices and producing limited size, usually single-family residential architecture so far, have received increasingly large scale commissions. Avant-garde architects, such as Ando, Ito, Hara, Hasegawa, Shinohara, Takeyama, Takamatsu, and many others, previously belonging to or representing an oppositional counter-culture, are now involved in such projects of national, even international significance, such as the Raika Headquarters in Osaka (1989) and the Himeji Children's Museum (1989) by Ando, the Yatsushiro Municipal Museum (1991) by Ito, the Iida City Museum (1988) and the New Kyoto Railroad Station (1994) by Hara, the Shonandai Cultural Centre (1991) by Hasegawa, the Tokyo International Port Terminal (1991) by Takeyama, or the Kunibiki Messe in Shimane Prefecture (1993) by Takamatsu. These projects among others are produced, of course, in addition to the numerous ones turned out by the offices of an older generation of internationally long-time reputable architects: Maki, Isozaki, Kurokawa, etc.

Although the majority of architectural output may be the design and realisation of commercial facilities, as the above list proves, there is an impressively large and fast growing number of cultural complexes; museums, conference and exposition centres, exhibition galleries, sports facilities and, very importantly, a new type of public housing or residential architecture in Japan. All these new projects in rapid succession have attracted public attention and increased the reputation of architecture not only with their sheer number and the genuine demand for them, but also by their quality, the often bold and experimental nature of their design, not to mention the high-level craftsmanship, detailing, and overall execution that have shaped them all through. In this respect it is not an overstatement to say that the most forward-looking or future-oriented architecture comes from Japan today; in Japan the future is now. This much is implicitly acknowledged also by many of the growing number of admirers of contemporary Japanese design, such as the British architect Peter Cook, who recently asked: 'Where do we go for the most important architectural information? At the moment, I think that is Japan.'[11]

In Japan today, there is another yet not entirely new way of forwarding the cause of architecture. Several real estate companies or developers now act as enlightened promoters of large, urban-scale projects. Some of these ventures have their obvious precedent in the 1927 exhibition of Modernist model housing, the Weissenhof-siedlung in Stuttgart, Germany (organised and partially designed by Mies van der Rohe while sponsored by the Deutscher Werkbund), and more recently in the Internationale Bauausstellung Berlin (IBA) of 1987. Among the larger ones of such undertakings in Japan, the Nexus World Kashii, and Seaside Momochi, both in Fukuoka city, should be mentioned. In both cases these housing projects were carried out with the purpose of introducing new models of common living to the Japanese. In order to do so, the developers appointed well-known Japanese architects as both designers and commissioners.

Isozaki, who was also the producer of Nexus, became the chief engineer behind this project with Hajime Yatsuka acting as director. Upon their agreement with the developer Fukuoka Jisho, they invited numerous foreign architects, in addition to a couple of Japanese ones, to participate. Steven Holl, Rem Koolhaas, Mark Mack, Christian de Portzamparc and Oscar Tusquets have designed one building each, while Osamu Ishiyama, adding a small group of residential blocks of his own, has represented Japan in the international cast. Isozaki himself has contributed to the medium, six- to ten-storey high housing project with a pair of highrise towers: a cylindrical and a rectangular one, connected by a bridge-like passage on the 30th level some 100m above the ground. This more than 30-storey-high tower complex, somewhat reminiscent of its prototype, the World Trade Centre in New York, is to accommodate 400 apartment units when the construction is completed in 1993. The smaller scale and also architecturally less successful Seaside Momochi was designed by another group of both foreign (Michael Graves, Stanley Tigerman, etc) and Japanese (Kisho Kurokawa, Shoei Yoh, etc) architects.

More unusual, however, in its conception is the ongoing Kumamoto Artpolis, a large-scale architectural and urban project sponsored by the Kumamoto prefectural government. Within this programme, initiated by the previous governor of Kumamoto, Morihiro Hosokawa in 1988, the commissioner is again Isozaki who, with the continued help of Yatsuka, invited a large number of prominent Japanese and a selected group of foreign architects to participate. The programme here is considerably larger than in any of the previously mentioned Japanese or foreign projects. Yet, what makes Kumamoto Artpolis unparalleled is the fact that on the one hand, the programme is not limited to Kumamoto city alone but extended to include even the most remote areas of the whole prefecture; on the other hand it is not a one-time project, but a continuous undertaking with new facilities commissioned annually. Within this programme, the already built and yet to be commissioned and designed individual buildings or complexes are not always grouped together, but are scattered in both urban and rural areas with the expectation of having a positive impact on the public awareness and the development of many parts of the prefecture, including small communities.

Now, after more than 50 projects completed, under construction, and/or commissioned, the project is not only well under way, but is also revealing manifest signs of its remarkable success. The Artpolis project has already yielded numerous outstanding pieces of architecture often with significant implications for, or visions of, a new urbanism. Among these, Ito's Yatsushiro Municipal Museum (1991), Shinohara's North Police Station (1990), Sejima's Saishunkan Dormitory (1991), and again, several housing projects, such as Yamamoto's Hotakubo, Hayakawa's Shinchi, plus the Takuma Housing, designed by Sakamoto, Hasegawa, and Matsunaga come to mind first. Also, Ando's Forest of Tombs Museum, to be completed in 1992, promises to be one of the best representatives of both the Artpolis and his own recently unfolding new architecture. Since its inception, the Kumamoto Artpolis has been serving as a model for several other prefectures, which are now in the process of devising their own similar projects.

All these and other new developments in architecture and urbanism, needless to say, are extensively featured, discussed and disseminated as celebrated events in Japanese journals, magazines, even daily papers, and frequently on the TV screens. With architecture becoming a trendy topic, many architects are now also being turned into and treated as 'pop stars' or fashion designers by the media. This is a phenomenon, however, that is not limited to Japan, but characterises the international scene of architecture in general. Moreover, just as much as Japanese publications have always followed with keen interest the architectural events in foreign countries, nowadays there is also an increased interest in and coverage of Japanese architecture in the media abroad, yielding this way a growing flow of information exchange among the architects of the globe. Indeed, our age of information has effectively

Tadao Ando, Children's Museum, Hyogo, Himeji

Nexus World Kashii, Housing development model, Fukuoka

Kazuo Shinohara, North Police Headquarters, Kumamoto

Riken Yamamoto, Hotakubo Public Housing, Kumamoto

ushered in an era of globalisation in the world of architecture as well.

Japan on the International Scene

As a result of the growing influence of the media and the overall process of globalisation, more and more Western architects are invited to build in Japan while the number of Japanese designers working on projects from abroad has risen sharply in recent years. Kurokawa, like Tange, has for some time been busy building in many countries; yet now, in the role of representing Japan abroad, he is joined by such other internationally acclaimed designers as Isozaki, Maki, Ando, Shinohara, Takamatsu, Ito, etc. Isozaki's MOCA in Los Angeles (1986), San Jordi Sports Arena in Barcelona (1990), and Disney World Headquarters Building in Florida (1991) are among his best recent works. Ando's unique Japan Pavilion for the World Fair in Seville has just been completed, while Maki's project for the Yerba Buena Gardens Visual Arts Centre in San Francisco is under construction. Shinohara and Takamatsu are working on large scale projects, both in France; the former on a hotel in Lille (1994), the latter on a cultural centre in Dijon (1995). Furthermore, Takamatsu has also opened a branch office in Berlin, Germany this year.

More phenomenal is the fast-growing number of foreign architects working on various projects in Japan, and it appears that their success in promoting new architecture far exceeds that of many foreign businessmen in selling their products. The Japanese have always been fascinated by and borrowed from the architectural culture of other nations all through history. As early as the mid-7th century AD, Chinese builders and craftsmen were active in the country and helped to build Buddhist temples, monasteries, etc. Then later, after the Meiji restoration, numerous foreign experts, including architects and engineers, were invited to establish the foundations of 'modern' Western architecture and teach the first generation of Japanese 'professional' designers. After the turn of the century, Frank Lloyd Wright, Antonin Raymond, and later Le Corbusier worked in Japan for shorter or longer periods of time. These architects had a more or less demonstrable impact on the course of Japanese architecture.[12] After the war, however, when Japan was rebuilding the country and the entire infrastructure, and even later on, the interest of foreign architects in Japan was by and large limited to its traditional architecture, while contemporary developments were regarded as remote curiosities– esoteric phenomena that could work in Japan but would be largely irrelevant in the West. Nevertheless, it was the 'incoherent' and 'unstable' contemporary built landscape that Westerners understood the least and despised the most. Foreigners working in Japan or on Japanese projects in the 60s and 70s were practically unheard of.

In the late 1980s this attitude has changed drastically. Not only is Japanese architecture now considered as being on the cutting edge of international developments, but also more and more foreign architects have the incentive as well as the opportunity to work in Japan. Practically every international star of architecture has one or more work completed or under construction in Tokyo, Osaka, Fukuoka, and elsewhere in the country. Eisenman,

Botta, Rossi, Gehry, Foster, Graves, Holl, Koolhaas, Morphosis, Portzamparc, and many others are now active in Japan. Some, like Zaha Hadid, have completed their first work here.

With such a surge of foreigners in Japan there are obvious questions to ask, for example, what kind of architecture are these visitors able to produce in Japan or, more precisely, how is the quality of their work affected by working in the Japanese *milieu* ; and, conversely, what kind of impact do their projects have on the Japanese? In general, these 'foreign' works have benefitted from their architects' collaboration with local firms or ateliers which prepared the working-drawings and construction documents. As a result, architectural details and finishes, for which the Japanese are famous, are superbly elaborated, resolved, and flawlessly executed thereby contributing in most cases significantly to the quality of these designs. Eisenman's Koizumi Lighting Theatre produced jointly with Kojiro Kitayama, in Tokyo (1990) or Aldo Rossi's Hotel Il Palazzo in Fukuoka (1989) are among the best examples.

Furthermore, some of these designers seem to have been able to adjust 'better' to the unusual and – for most of them – difficult local conditions, codes, regulations, etc, that is to say, the Japanese context in general, while others have been less successful in this regard. This is so to the extent that some, like Holl, Eisenman, Rossi, and Morphosis have reached or even surpassed the quality of design they are individually recognised for on the international scene. Steven Holl's apartment complex in Nexus World, Fukuoka, for example, is arguably his most significant or best work to date. Others however, notably Botta, Graves, Tigerman, and Gehry's works are less convincing, falling short of expectations.

Yet, there is another issue to comment upon in regard to the growing number of works by foreign architects in Japan. It is the inevitable tendency with which these designers bring their own unmistakable vision of architecture and urbanism into play on the Japanese scene; or it is the issue of how they intend, are able, or sometimes, how far they *have* to respond to the 'peculiarity' of the Japanese cultural and urban context. The often required use of tatami flooring in rooms and many other elements that the Japanese, despite their globalised contemporary culture, have retained as part of their mode of living is a case in point. Aldo Rossi's Hotel Il Palazzo, for instance, features numerous Japanese style rooms and premises in addition to the four bars that have been designed by the Japanese Shiro Kuramata as well as other foreign interior designers. The Hotel, however, exemplifies another aspect of the 'unreal' situation that most foreign works incite or reinforce in Japan; Rossi, with the Il Palazzo, has actually deployed a fragment of his rigorously rational model for the Classical Italian city, which now finds itself randomly superimposed on the 'chaotic' texture of the Japanese urbanscape. In other words, Rossi, with his implicitly nostalgic and alien model, has created what Maki calls a '"meta-contextual" topos' in the indiscriminately mingled Japanese urban environment where every building embodies its own vision of the city.[13] A radical juxtaposition characterises Eisenman's Koizumi building as well, although the project has obviously nothing to do with Classicism at all.

Yet, Rem Koolhaas, in his many ways innovative residential complex at Nexus, Fukuoka, has felt compelled to pay homage to the notion of 'Japaneseness' by wrapping his two buildings in bands of fake rough-stone walls – actually made of black painted concrete – reminiscent of the ramparts of medieval Japanese castles. The effect in all these cases is rather hallucinatory, and as such undermines a person's sense of reality. This is further reinforced, particularly in the Nexus World project, by the random heterogeneity of the designs relative not only to the Japanese environment, but also to one another. Therefore, more than the quality of the individual elements, as Yatsuka has correctly observed, 'What is at issue [here], is this randomness, which was made possible only in this age of globalisation and the electronic media.'[14] No doubt, Japan has by now become not merely an 'integral' part of, but also a leading or driving force behind the fast growing worldwide or global network of our accelerated contemporary architectural production as well. As a result, it is now increasingly difficult even for the Japanese to define their own identity and the 'real' nature of their culture. The raising of the question, therefore, as to what extent it is still possible to talk about a specifically Japanese architecture, is justified.

Experiments in Schizophrenic Uncertainty

The runaway architectural culture in Japan has produced an urban environment that, as observed in its extreme, virtually borders on the schizophrenic. Behind the overall context of such developments today, most architects recognise, although do not necessarily endorse, the all-encompassing processes of commercialisation and the onslaught of information or media technology on the entire society. It is clear for them that the unleashed realm of this urban environment, in conjunction with its 'mental landscape' that it instigates – now free from all but the frenzy of human desires – is increasingly impossible not only to control, but also escape; their work is inevitably part of the scenario. As the 'hermeticist' trends of the 1970s proved, a radically confrontational or adversary attitude could be effectively pre-empted by the totalising forces of the delirious Japanese commodity and media culture.

In the 1990s, it seems that architects have no real choice but to accept the Japanese city as is, or as virtual reality. Therefore, the new architecture in Japan more than before is paradoxical and in certain instances as schizophrenic as the cultural and built landscape in which it is set. Although it is undeniable that Japan's unprecedentedly accelerated urban culture has rendered the fate of architecture both literally and semantically unpredictable, it has also opened up almost unlimited possibilities, in fact the demand, for innovative, experimental designs that, in most cases, can be characterised by a sense for both realism and fiction. The astonishingly broad spectrum of architectural intentions and directions therefore should be considered and eventually evaluated with regard to how Japanese architects understand and are able to respond to the interrelationship between reality and fiction. In so doing, however, there is no way of avoiding a 'substantial' re-evaluation and redefinition of the parameters and the very 'essence' of architecture and the city.

Monumentality Versus the Simulated City and Nature

One such parameter is the quality of monumentality that is the perceived need or role of monuments in the contemporary city, versus nature and ephemerality. There are few other issues today that have polarised Japanese designers so drastically as this one. At one end of the scale are those who are adamant on the need of monumental architecture and, in certain cases, like Tange's, also of a highly ordered urbanism, in order to forcefully anchor the dizzyingly volatile, but often also appealingly phenomenal realm of the city. At the other end of the scale, then, are those who question the validity and even the possibility of monumentality, and experiment with the ephemeral in architecture. In between the two extremes the gradations are numerous, and even among those who follow the traits of a new monumentalism towards another reality, the differences in design can be and are enormous. To exemplify, the works of Kenzo Tange and Shin Takamatsu come to mind.

Both Tange and Takamatsu have been, from the beginning of their careers, pursuing an architecture wherein monumentality is one of the most important features of design. Yet Tange, rejecting categorically the messy ambiguity and, by extension, also much of the vitality of the Japanese city as he has always done, continues to insist on a preconceived, rational model of architecture and urbanism with an unimpeachable reality, whose impossibility or meaninglessness in the present state of both society and the metropolis he fails to see. His new Tokyo City Hall of 1991, as with many of his recent works, is an unmistakable example of an anachronistically heroic and ultimately futile gesture that astounds one with its pretentious 'imperial' grandeur and uniformly rigid composition, a composition that has its apparent prototype in Western medieval religious structures.

Like Gothic cathedrals denoting spiritual authority and the centre of urban life, Tange's intention must have been to symbolise the authority of the metropolitan government while creating an unquestionably meaningful urban centre. Yet, with public life and space now being 'decentred' or dispersed, gravitating inevitably to commercial, communication, transportation and many other 'centres', Tange's authoritarian design, paradoxically, can only frame and stage a highly controlled, even oppressive and totalitarian urban reality that is overshadowed by the political power of the State. Furthermore, as Yatsuka has pointed out: 'In a highly developed consumer society where distinctions between ruler and ruled have virtually ceased to exist, the State is no longer a consolidated identity requiring the support of strong visual imagery.'[15] Indeed, Tange with his new City Hall seems to have missed the point – and the 'centre' which had already been historically destroyed.

Tange's historicising and dogmatic monumentality can be contrasted with Takamatsu's non-historicist, enigmatic and highly-sensuous monumental designs. While profoundly frustrated by the hopelessness of the urban conditions in which they are conceived yet intend to fight, they actually seem to both contribute to and benefit from the very conditions. His works embody the monumental aesthetics of some mysterious, precision-crafted and

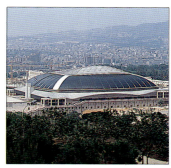

Arata Isozaki, Sant Jordi Sports Hall, Barcelona

Arata Isozaki, Disneyworld Headquarters, Orlando, Florida

Steven Holl, Nexus World Kashii Housing, Tokyo

Aldo Rossi, Hotel 'Il Palazzo', Fukuoka

over-scaled mechanical models, or rather, ritualistic objects, whose extreme intensity of expression trying to overpower and outrun everything around is meant to compensate for the impossibility of architecture's future in the city; they are as surreal as the vast sea of the restless urbanscape on which they float. Like 'hollowed out' and fragmented shells ('shipwrecks'), deprived of any possible destination, Takamatsu's buildings, such as the Syntax and Solaris for example, while apparently participating in the orgy of a strangely gay urban celebration, actually and paradoxically, can only signify some uniquely bizarre memorials that are dedicated to either the 'death of the monument,' or the 'death of the city,' or perhaps both.[16]

In other words, Tange's monumental architecture is driven by the designer's naive optimism rooted in bourgeois positivism, while Takamatsu's by his desperate pessimism bordering on outright nihilism. Takamatsu's architecture, however, is in the process of changing, and so, many of his most recent projects such as the Zeus, a small museum of sand in Shimane (1991), the Yamanaka Onsen Hotel (1993), the Sunset Cathedral, another museum in Yamagata (1993), the Toyako Hotel (1994), and most especially the Kunibiki Messe, also in Shimane (1993), do point towards a new, perhaps less stage-set or object-like monumentality that, while not without some continued heterogeneity and the quality of science-fiction, is calmer and aspires as much to the cosmic and the phenomenal as it does to the scientific/technological in architecture.

With respect to monumentality, recent works of Shinohara, Isozaki, Takeyama, and even Ando have to be mentioned as further examples that broaden the scope in various directions. The line of design initiated by Shinohara in his 1987 TIT Centennial Hall introduced a kind of techno-monumentality or the monumentality of the 'zero degree machine'. His architecture's powerful yet accidental formal disposition, that finds as much affinity as dissimilarity with the 'random noise' of urban reality, is also the outcome of applying incongruous structural systems. This is further elaborated in the huge hotel he is designing for the city of Lille in France. Such incongruity, however, is not only a conceptual response to the city, but as his K-2 Office Building in Osaka proves, it is also often an unavoidable precondition dictated by the disorderly urban site; the K-2 Building thus tends towards the schizophrenic.

Isozaki pushes this direction to the extreme. Signs of surrealism have always been present in his architecture, yet this quality, enhanced by a fascination with incongruity, took on a more explicit form in the 'suspended monumentality' of the Tsukuba Centre Building (1983), and has continued with varying intensity in his works thereafter. (Comparing the Tsukuba with the new Tokyo City Hall and the majority of Takamatsu's architecture can respectively reveal important disparities and also some interesting similarities in their designs.) In the recent Art Tower Mito (1990), Isozaki's monumentality has reached an unmistakably schizophrenic level. The strongly historicising, Classicist volumes surrounding a small courtyard plaza, are juxtaposed with the 100-metre-high spiralling, metallic and futuristic structure of the tower that, clad in shiny titanium plates, and surging from the green courtyard as a mesmerising mirage, lends the whole complex and the small town beyond, an ambience of astonishing unreality. The Art Tower, as much as most of Takamatsu's work, underscores the paradox that, in the post-urban/post-ideal society, where architecture is deprived of all its native context and conventions, 'the urban monument, (in order) to be effective . . . must be out of place.'[17]

Minoru Takeyama's new Tokyo Port Terminal adds yet another dimension to the articulation of urban monument. Having been landed on an artificial, reclaimed site in Tokyo bay, it is, in a sense, also out of place. Yet this specific location at the margins of the city and the sea have provided further aspects to play important roles in the design. Inspired by the spirit of Constructivism and Japanese Metabolism, the Terminal manifests a certain structural monumentalism. Yet this monumentality is impressively challenged, transformed and occasionally even defused by the sensibility with which the building engages its natural environment. The screen-like structural frame that envelops the upper sections, the large, Teflon-fibre domes and other canopies, plus the fluidity of spaces all imbue the design with a quality of the phenomenal.

As Ando's popularity and national, plus international, reputation have rapidly grown throughout the years so have the number and size of his commissions. Today, far from designing only small residences or residential architecture, he also works on churches, museums, theatres, large commercial complexes, etc. With the continued, almost exclusive reliance on massive, exposed reinforced concrete structures, the increased size inevitably raises the issue of monumentality in his architecture. As a matter of fact, a certain degree of this quality has always characterised Ando's works. His early residences, determined to defend their inhabitants from the invasion of the deteriorating urban conditions, were conceived in an ideology and architecture which, while making a powerful resistive stance of their own, yielded a 'minimalist' monumentalism. It is also safe to say that for Ando such a rejection of the contemporary city has been channelled into his larger, urban-scale projects as well. And so, some of his recent complexes, such as the Children's Museum in Himeji (1989), the Raika Headquarters in Osaka (1990) and, to a lesser degree, the Museum of Literature, also in Himeji (1990), manifest apparent monumentality.

What offsets this tendency here and in the best of Ando's designs is his exceptional capability to perceptually 'dematerialise' the heavy structural corporeality of his architecture. Mobilising natural phenomena in provocative yet profoundly poetic ways, Ando can render the limited, material reality of a rational architecture into a phenomenally rich spatial experience that is as concrete as it is ephemeral and is evocative of the spiritual. The most representative of such spiritual quality are, of course, the small chapels on Mount Rokko (1986), in Hokkaido (1988) and in Osaka (1989), all Christian churches that are, conspicuously, located in natural landscapes away from large urban areas. The recent addition to his ecclesiastic architecture, the Water Temple on Awaji Island (1991) – the first Buddhist religious structure by him – is the latest and perhaps most powerful testament to Ando's artistry. In a way similar to that of Buddhist thought and conduct he expands reality's horizon by encompassing the worlds of emotions and the ephemeral.

One aspect of the Water Temple's design, however, is new in Ando's architecture; the building is almost entirely buried underground. In order to descend into this subterranean world, one has to enter through the large, oval dish-like roof covered with a pool of water. Only one small corner of the temple space below cuts through the sloping ground to let in the light of the setting sun. Visible above ground, beyond the reflective surface of the water, are only two concrete walls: one curving, the other straight; they guide visitors to the entrance.

While the gesture of extending architecture into the earth has been frequently used by Ando in his previous projects, the extent of architecture's 'disappearance', along with a new approach to monumentality, is certainly unparalleled here. Ando seems to explore this approach further in other projects: the Forest of Tombs Museum in Kumamoto (1991), and the Chikatsu Asuka Museum in Osaka (1994). Although none of them is completely underground, their designs strongly allude to the idea, insofar as they are shaped as the earthwork of large, ancient burial mounds that surround them, and the culture of which they intend to introduce. These museums, particularly the one in Osaka, have in effect become extensions of their sloping and undulating sites; comprised largely of a series of wide stairways, ramps and stepped platforms, from which visitors can observe the mounds, the horizontally stretching structures emerge gradually, almost 'unnoticeably' from the ground. Much of the exhibition spaces are arranged below ground and are dark, imparting the feeling of being inside a tomb.

In his Nakanoshima Project (1988), an urban park proposal for downtown Osaka, the extensive cultural facilities – an art museum, conference hall, concert hall, etc are again all underground, thereby reserving the areas above ground for the park: greenery, landscaping and open air facilities. The motif of a wide open stairway also returns here, to mediate between the river and the island as well as the park and the architecture below. These new projects by Ando seem to indicate, partially at least, a shift in direction within his architecture both literally and figuratively. His new line is suggestive of an architectural 'silence' by way of architecture's self-effacement and so, while pointing away from monumentality, coincides momentarily with the intentions of some of his contemporaries: Aida, Takamatsu and even Ito.[18] It is surprising to discover, for example, that, despite the obvious major differences in their architectures, how much Takamatsu's stairstepped, podium-like design for the Sunset Cathedral Museum and Ando's Chikatsu-Asuka Museum share in common. Moreover, Ito in some of his recent projects also experiments with burying or covering parts of architecture with earth. All this proves that architects of different ideological convictions, working in dissimilar design paradigms, can and do have points of intersection in their lines of architecture.

What emerges from the examples discussed above, in relation to architecture's continued attempt to define and also transform its own reality, is the reconsidered and new roles of *nature* and the outside world. True, Ando and many others have, throughout the years, consistently relied on nature's evocative power often in such cramped urban situations where the natural environment had already been totally squeezed out by reckless developments. Yet, with the situation in cities not really improving, there are several new attempts to engage or evoke nature with or within architecture, and now this may also happen away from urban areas.

Ryoji Suzuki's House in Sagi is a poignant example for the broadening of design response to the 'natural'. In addition to taking full advantage of direct views of the sea and the sky, there are several initiatives to move away from the single perspective of a fixed viewpoint. Suzuki's design, as with most of his works, is another experiment in shifting human experience away from the static towards the motional. What he calls 'experience in material' is an attempt to probe into the material reality of experience, using here various techniques of framing, superimposing, reflecting, and other transformations of vistas, while inciting movement in order to materialise the immaterial and vice versa. In his buildings, therefore, there is always a close connection between motion and emotion as well as the concrete and the phenomenal or illusory.

Another way of engaging the environment today is the reinterpretation and increased use of 'topography'. Starting with Hara and Yamamoto, numerous architects in the late 1980s began to interpret the existing fabric of the 'city as topography' and build over or above this reality.[19] Their projects are frequently articulated with two different realms: one that as an infill provides the continuity of the [urban] landscape, the other, landing on this substratum, embodies the new architecture and often a new, miniature city.

Much of this architecture acts then as an artificial land on which urban activity could continue while giving way to the 'independently' shaped and working, new facilities above. Such 'simulated' lands with another architecture on them, in reality, mean structures that are designed with extensive, directly-accessible rooftop terraces, plazas, intricate walkways, stairs, parks, gazebos and other sceneries that interweave the whole complex. The Iida City Museum and Sotetsu Cultural Centre by Hara, the Tokyo International Port Terminal by Takeyama, and, to some degree, even the Syntax by Takamatsu are good examples of this approach. In her Shonandai Cultural Centre, Hasegawa goes a step further, insofar as she, along with her intentions to articulate 'architecture as another nature', has defined the majority of the Centre in the forms of not only the land and 'rolling hills' but also of 'natural' sceneries with symbolic trees and woods.[20]

However, we can observe the emergence of a trend which, rather than interpreting architecture as landscape or nature, approaches and utilises the landscape as architecture. Perhaps the first attempt of this is identifiable in Yasumitsu Matsunaga's 'Inscription' House of 1987. Here on the relatively flat terrain a bulwark of earth is used to shape as well as cover parts of the architecture. Ando's Water Temple, more than his other works, is another step in this direction. Ito's two recent projects: the Sapporo Beer Guest House (1989) and the Yatsushiro Municipal Museum are more explicit in their intention. With large parts of their structures buried under berms of earth, both of these buildings create a new relationship between architecture and the material reality of the land. Not unlike some of

Peter Eisenman, Koizumi Lighting Building, Tokyo

Rem Koolhaas, Nexus World Kashii Housing, Fukuoka

Kenzo Tange, New Tokyo City Hall

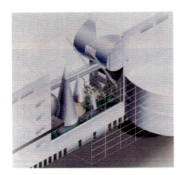

Shin Takamatsu, Kunibiki Messe, detail of the 'Garden of Abstract Forms'

Kazuo Shinohara, TIT Centennial Hall, Tokyo

Tadao Ando, Raika Headquarters, Osaka

Emilio Ambasz's projects, in Ito's Guest House and Museum the earthwork is neither really landscaping nor gardening as something created in addition to architecture, but is an active part of building. At the same time, it can also be interpreted as a mode of questioning architecture's present image of reality and material monumentality.

In other examples, and on a much smaller scale, the 'architecturalisation of landscape' continues within the realm of architecture itself. This is evidenced in tiny courtyards that are sunken or sloped into the ground; Ando has designed residential as well as commercial complexes, including the Collezione, with subterranean courts or small plazas. Atsushi Kitagawara in his Metroca and Santo projects, moves into the ground to create small landscapes that are both real light courts and, as he himself admits, fictive scenarios, urbanscapes or landscapes, insofar as the first is a 'micro spatial city', whereas the second a 'micro garden' for which Kyoto – where the Santo is located – with its myriad of tiny gardens, is famous for.[21] Finally, Suzuki, in his Kounji Zen Temple – which, not unlike Ando's Water Temple, is sunken into the ground almost in its entirety – models his 'internalised landscapes' on the dynamics of the 'Void of Missing Link', wherein void is the chaotic network of gaps that interweave Japanese cities in a most astonishing way.[22]

Nevertheless, the truly opposite direction to a monumental architecture is pursued by architects whose designs are comprised of almost no material substance. With a reality constituted largely by the environment in which they are set and which in turn imbues them, the 'essence' of these lightweight structures is not only related to natural and other phenomena, but in effect also evoked by them. Appearing as if being only temporary shelters, designs such as Ito's own house, the Silver Hut (1984), House in Magomezawa (1985), Nomad Pub (1986), the Ueda Art Gallery (1991) and many others by Ito, as well as Sejima's Platform Houses (1988 and 90), Hasegawa's House in Nerima (1986) and many others by her or Sakamoto, etc, aspire to the ephemeral.

From New Technologies to a New Space
Today's design intentions, to mediate between, or contrast with the realities of architecture and nature and/or the world at large, now increasingly rely on new technologies that include the latest in construction, computer and media technologies. This tendency also signals the emergence of a new modernism or the return of 'Modernism with a difference'. The range of examples wherein a new approach to technology is particularly evident, includes the work of such diverse designers as Shinohara, Isozaki, Maki, Hara, Hasegawa, Ito, Sakamoto, Sejima, Yatsuka, Kitagawara and, very importantly, Takamatsu. Indeed, as their respective architectures betray, these architects reinterpret technology in their own individual ways, and also according to the unique character or demand of the task at hand. Yet, despite the differences among them, these interpretations share some important common features that set them far apart from their Modernist counterparts.

The difference stems first of all from the ability of new technologies to go far beyond the confines of a structural, material (corporeal) reality inscribed in and by the instrumental logic and productive rationality of previous Modernism. Modernism, the product of the 'first machine age', was preoccupied primarily with rational systematisation, standardisation, mass production, industrialisation or, in short, with industrial technology which was, by nature, profoundly universal. In other words, Modernism was driven and riding on a technology of hardware as represented by the mechanism and function of the idealised Machine. Such preoccupation eventually led to the anonymity of architecture and the impoverishment of the built environment. Modernism, in spite of many revolutionary achievements, has lost its momentum and opened itself to just criticism.

On the other hand, the range of new technologies behind today's developments in architecture and culture is more akin to a software technology that operates like a computer programme run with 'fuzzy logic'. With no claim to universality and rigid rationality, this technology is more intuitive, flexible, more locally inflected or episodic, and is capable of addressing – as well as generating – contradictory conditions; its aim is to engender *milieu* or mood by stimulating all the human senses, albeit often not without prompting a new awareness as well. This technology, as manifested in the resulting architecture, although engaging the speculative mind, intends to appeal more importantly to human emotions and desires, and in so doing, it is often explicitly sensual. Tectonic considerations do continue to play important roles in most cases, but not without a vastly increased emphasis on appearances: surfaces, details and parts that, now often rendered autonomous, are conducive to fragmented constructs and landscapes where the 'whole' remains always an elusive phenomenon. The new technologies now can and do open new perspectives towards and broaden the horizon of architectural and human reality but, far more than before, they can also simulate and control these realities; they represent tremendous potentials for human experience and reality, yet at the same time also hugely increase the risk of generating merely pseudo-experience.

The potentials and impact of the new 'software' technologies are far-reaching in architecture as much as elsewhere, and it is evident that in Japan these potentials are being thoroughly explored in a growing number of directions with both their positive and negative implications. Such directions would include five distinct aspects in contemporary design: a new role of tectonics, high-tech craftsmanship, theatricality, industrial vernacular or neo-primitivism and, finally, a spectacular phenomenalism. Many of these aspects, although seemingly paradoxical, even mutually exclusive in Modernist understanding, are mobilised and appear together, while occasionally also enhancing one another, in the very same designs. New structural solutions, for example, are often forwarded along articulate detailing and phenomenal craftsmanship; tectonics plays an important role in bringing about a new industrial vernacular; primitivism often allies itself with the phenomenal; while detailing and craftsmanship can engender a manifest theatricality on the one hand, and the quality of the ephemeral on the other.[23]

A survey of recent output in Japanese architecture reveals that frequently the unique qualities of new designs are directly related to a particular emphasis on and/or novel articulation of *tectonics*. In this respect, the consistency of Ando's architecture is a well-known case in point, and so is Shoei Yoh's, whose entire architectural enterprise is devoted to the expressive structural possibility of design; one of his latest projects, the Saibu Gas Museum in Fukuoka (1989), is an excellent representative of this pursuit. Numerous other examples have already been mentioned; among them: Takeyama's Port Terminal (1991), Isozaki's Tower within the Mito Art Complex (1990), etc. Another outstanding recent structure by Isozaki is his spectacular San Jordi Sports Arena in Barcelona (1990). Both the Tower and the Arena are designed with very special structural systems. Achievements of both virtuoso architectural design and engineering bravura, the tectonic articulation of these buildings greatly contributes to their dramatic impact.

One of Maki's several recent experiments in innovative structural systems, the Tokyo Metropolitan Gymnasium (1990) joins the two projects by Isozaki; it too derives its highly-surrealistic appearance from tectonics. Enhanced by the quality of employed materials and surface treatment, the experience of these designs is akin to that of a mirage; they are evocative of the sublime. On the other hand, Shinohara's application of heterogeneous structural frames and systems, as in his TIT Centennial Hall (1987) and K-2 Building (1990) produce fragmentary compositions that have no 'stable' reality. Aida's long-standing experimentation with systems of fragmented concrete walls continues in his Saito Memorial Hall, yielding a visual experience, what he calls *yuragi* or fluctuation.[24]

Hiromi Fujii, who otherwise shares no common ideological background with Aida, is even more committed to 'animating' structural walls thereby departing wilfully from a taken-for-granted architectural reality. Often rendered as independent screens, his walls are intersected by others, rotated, tilted, etc; they seem to be in the process of some dynamic transformation producing forms and spaces that have in Fujii's words 'escaped the confines of our world'.[25] Two small residential projects, the Mizoe 1 and 2 (1988 and 1991) illustrate these qualities well. What is unusual in all of these designs is the mode in which the structural system, beyond providing the buildings' physical stability, also brings about their perceptual instability. In other words, as in the case of Modernist architecture, tectonics plays a visibly important role in shaping these buildings, yet the result, rather than being a unified, rationally integrated whole as with the Modernists, tends to be a *fragmentary*, collaged and 'uncertain form', or almost no 'form' at all. This latter is particularly evidenced by examples such as Ito's Sapporo Beer Guest House or Sejima's Platform 2, where the structure disappears or approximates the 'lightness of virtual immateriality'.

Beyond the unique formal articulation of structures, the effect of new technologies is also apparent, and perhaps even more so, in the articulation of details, surfaces, etc, not to say anything about the application of a vastly broadened spectrum of industrially produced materials. This tendency represents a new standard in high quality *craftsmanship*, a craftsmanship that does not exhaust itself in merely good or even perfect functional solutions;

often it goes far beyond. The attention and care going into certain elaborations or detailings on every scale, including the 'micro' dimension, or the precision with which some of the buildings are put together seem to defy any material, productional and constructional limitation. This is an attitude and quality that – within the scope of the latest contemporary technologies of course – parallel or 'surpass' the artistry of traditional craftsmen.

Such preoccupation with detailing can be contrasted again with the manifest shortcomings of previous Modernist design and building, wherein details were often regarded as some kind of unnecessary luxury. Exceptions notwithstanding, Modernist architecture could be characterised either by a lack of detailing or a crudeness of details that added to, or outright generated the monotony of design. Treating unfinished concrete structures is one example. Modern buildings of this material, even at their best, were frequently 'plagued' with imprecisions, rough surfaces and a brutality of appearance. Ando's first projects in the early 1970s, for instance, were still displaying some of these qualities, but over the years he has been unfailingly perfecting both design and technology; today his walls and frames, despite their size, impress one, with an utmost precision of form and detail, delicacy of texture, plus a smoothness and reflective quality of surfaces, that render the unfinished concrete a luscious matter, capable of perceptually challenging its own material substance.

Maki's handling and articulating aluminium panels and stainless-steel sheeting is another excellent case in point. He applied stainless steel as roof cover for the first time on his Fujisawa Municipal Gymnasium (1984). To achieve the graphic texture of roof surfaces, the contractor had to invent a special machine with which workers could do the seams in a particular way. During the test runs, however, it turned out that no matter how much care was taken, the process of seaming up the thin stainless steel wrinkled the sheets in an unpredictable way. This problem was finally solved through repeated experiments in which the sheets were pre-wrinkled to a desirable degree before 'stitching' them together inch by inch along numerous yet delicately patterned seam lines.[26] The indefatigable efforts have paid off; the technology has since also been applied to Maki's other large projects: the Makuhari Messe (1989) and the Tokyo Metropolitan Gym (1990).

Detailing, however, when done in excess and/or in an overly manneristic way, can induce a sense of the *theatrical*. Today such quality, albeit with a wide range of intensity, imbues a growing number of recent projects. Some of Maki's own works, such as the Kyoto National Museum of Modern Art (1986), the Spiral Building (1985), or the Tepia (1989) show a tendency in this direction. Isozaki's Art Tower Mito, and Kitakyushu International Conference Centre (1990), following his first experiment within the Tsukuba Centre Building (1983), are also good examples for an architectural 'stage set'. Moreover, Hasegawa's Shonandai Cultural Centre (1991), Hara's Yamato International (1987) and Iida City Museum (1988), Kitagawara's most recent projects, and Yatsuka's Wing Building (1991) as well represent an elusive theatricality insofar as they allude to various fictive scenarios, be they natural or urban.

Tadao Ando, Chapel on the Water, Tomamu, Hokkaido

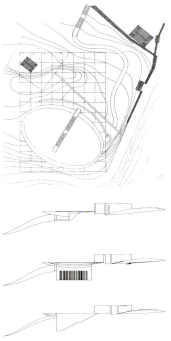

Tadao Ando, Water Temple, Awaji Island

Toyo Ito, 'Silver Hut', Tokyo

Itsuko Hasegawa, House in Nerima, Tokyo

None of these designs are devoid of an implicit predilection for the *ritualistic* in architecture. Yatsuka, continuing his line of fragmentary design, introduced it first in his Tarlazzi Building of 1987, arranged the Wing as an agglomeration of various parts, all rendered as signs. This building, perhaps more than any other discussed so far, demonstrates how materials, structures, and details can be rendered so as to acquire a curious autonomy relative to the whole. All these elements, if they are not already signs – like the large circular one above the stairway – are certainly on their way to become such signage. Yet, these are signs that have nothing particular to signify; they, similar to the wing-like canopies over the deep-cut crevice, simply float in a semantic space which, like the city around it, is in search of a destination. The building with its long, ritualistic open stairway in the sharply slit fissure, is akin to Piranesi's mythical/theatrical visions, yet, while the fragmentary world of this 18th-century artist is grandiose and heavy with the ruins of Classicism, Yatsuka's is light, drifting over the dismembered corps of Modernism.

Nonetheless, it is Takamatsu's designs which embody most a theatricality produced by the new technology. His buildings after the mid 1980s began to take the shape, image and, in certain cases, also the functioning of some curious high-tech machines replete with precision-crafted and meticulously-applied details. Quite obviously, Takamatsu's machines have nothing in common with the rational and functional 'machine' of Le Corbusier; rather, they assume the character and role of powerful ritualistic objects or devices that are as mystical and bizarre as they are irresistibly sensuous. These machines are intended and appear as 'desiring instruments' for the rituals of today's urban life, a life in which, paradoxically, rituals have already lost the object of their worship.

Most of the excessive details in Takamatsu's buildings: the heavy metallic parts, steel plates, highly polished surfaces, hinges, rods and the large rivets, etc, are technological in nature. Yet such details are only partially or, in most cases, not at all related to the actual architectural construction or to the modes of how the buildings work. Such details and elements therefore can only be, as they are, conducive to a pseudo-technology, or technology as merely an image; this is technology about technology itself or a form of *pop-tech*. With only populist and trivial contents, or no real content to signify and much less to symbolise, the Kirin, Syntax and Solaris, among others, can only produce another urban fiction, a fiction by way of 'technology'. In other words, all the busy details and elements that, as empty signs, crowd these buildings, are doomed to revolve around a hollow core, a metaphorical black hole, on the verge of inescapably being drawn into it.[27]

On the other hand, fictive scenarios in the city today are evoked not only by such 'meta-machines' as these over-scaled and robot-like constructs, but also by highly sophisticated apparatuses in conjunction with or in lieu of architecture. The Kirin Building (1987), also by Takamatsu, displays four gigantic towers of light whose flickering patterns are run by computers. The Kirin adds up to a kind of urban media show that extends the already saturated light-scape of the evening city, now 'alive' with huge, facade-size TV screens as well.

The 'performance' inside the multi-storey large space of Yoh's Saibu Gas Museum of Phenomenart expands the notion of 'architecture as media'. Visitors are treated to hourly shows complete with electronic music, digitalised sound effects and most extraordinary light effects. In the huge dark hall, a myriad of small light bulbs behind multi-layered, semi-transparent walls, floor and ceiling, flicker with the rhythm, transforming the interior space and architecture into a pulsating immaterial entity, a boundless multi-dimensional field wherein boundaries between the sensing human body and the world beyond disappear like dissipating mist. The experience, similar to the one of the contemporary city outside, is as stimulating as it is totally controlled, as fascinating and apparently liberating as it is frighteningly empty; it is the bleaching of any sense of reality by way of a direct sensory overload or manipulation. In this sense, the Kirin finds itself in close company with this museum of phenomenart.[28]

Two works by Hasegawa and Ito seem to continue such *high-tech phenomenalism*, but they also deviate from it in significant ways. Hasegawa's Shonandai Cultural Centre features various metallic screens shaped as canopies, 'foliage' or even trees. One of the latter is a 'tree of wind and light', another is with a built-in clock. There is a small light and music show played as the clockwork begins – on every hour – to rotate various parts of the 'tree'. This mechanical movement and media show are at least related to or indicative of the passing of time. At the same time the delicately layered perforated aluminium and other metallic screens are configured so as to be 'animated' by the natural light of the sun and the movement of the wind. In Hasegawa's words, they work as 'poetic machines'.[29]

Forging a link between the natural and the highly technological attains a particularly poignant expression in Ito's Tower of Wind (1986). Located in front of Yokohama Station, the tower is essentially the 'architectural camouflage' of a huge ventilation outlet for the underground shopping centre. The structure, wrapped around by several layers of semi-transparent acrylic layers and perforated aluminium screens in an oval shape, is rather inconspicuous during daytime. However, it comes alive in the evening, when the thousands of small light bulbs and neon lights, arranged among the surrounding layers, are lit. The system, working with a computer programme, monitors the various phenomena happening around and, through the changing patterns of flickering lights, displays the time of the day, the sound or noise level and, more importantly, the velocity and direction of wind. In the process, the tower itself, like a transparent film, is dematerialised, becoming visual environmental music.

Using various light effects as a means to 'break down' physical boundaries and modulate or expand space within the realm of illusion, has since become one area of investigation within Ito's design experiments. In the 'garden of light' of his Sapporo Beer Guest House project (1989), Ito has arranged numerous glass prisms that operate with liquid crystal (LC) inside; connected to the electric current of the sound system, these transparent volumes appear and disappear in a pulsating fashion along with the intensity of music, as the glass changes its transparency to 'frosted' white and back, and in so doing, produce a fascinatingly choreographed play.

In the Frankfurt Opera House interior (1991), in addition to systems of computer-controlled small lamps, directional lights, reflective and absorbing surfaces, Ito also used optical fibres above the perforated metal screen of the ceiling to create a kaleidoscopic effect. With this, the ceiling disappears, while the interior space appears to soar to cosmic dimension and quality. With changing the lighting pattern, however, various spatial experiences can be achieved. This is a theatre within the theatre, an illusion within another one. It is interesting to note that Ando's Urban Egg/Space Strata project, a 400-seat multi-purpose auditorium within his Nakanoshima Urban Park (1988) also features a spectacular lighting system that can be likened in effect to the examples above.

Moreover, Yasumitsu Matsunaga, in the four-storey lobby of his Y's Court Nakahara (1991), achieves the illusion of a cosmic space by way of mostly natural light. The curving surfaces of the vaulted ceiling and walls are punctured by numerous tiny roof lights and 'windows' that, while undermining one's sense of scale and distance, wash the atrium with the phenomenal, luminous immateriality of the diffuse light. Matsunaga's design then returns us to projects where, as opposed to entirely artificially generated or simulated worlds often in sealed interiors, the changing phenomena of the outside world – natural or urban – actively contribute to experiencing the illusive in relation to the real and vice versa. The Tower of Wind is a significant work in this respect; having very little material substance, the structure is essentially a system of thin, film-like layers which becomes 'architecturalised' by the act of responding to and displaying the events around. And, while this responsive mechanism here is provided through sophisticated computers, a growing number of other examples show that a similar sensibility can be achieved without the computer, although still relying on the benefits of new technologies.

New structures and materials, in conjunction with new modes of design, can now provide the possibility to construct or rather devise 'architecture' with an almost immaterial lightness and transparency. This architecture, aspiring if not to the physical then certainly to the perceptual impermanence of building, has brought about both a new *industrial vernacular,* and a new kind of space. Although many of the previously discussed works can be characterised by a certain illusive lightness, such qualities are brought home more poignantly by designs in which the application of new light-weight industrial materials and products are conducive to another kind of 'minimalist' simplicity, a simplicity which is not quite unlike the one underlying vernacular architecture.

Kazunari Sakamoto's Hoshida Common City Housing in Osaka (1991) attests to the fact that such industrial vernacular can create a convincing environment even on a large scale. The straightforward simplicity of the materials and construction makes the architecture here as real as the lightness of elements, reflectiveness and/or transparency of surfaces render it phenomenal. Riken Yamamoto's extensive but sensitive use of translucent Teflon-fibre tent structures and other 'floating' roofs or canopies over cavernous and airy semi-outdoor spaces – such as the

ones in his Hamlet, a residential complex (1988), as well as Matsunaga's application of simple materials and structures in his Forest Green Housing (1990), both in Tokyo – result in much the same attractive qualities and experiences.

On the other hand, in addition to using metallic structures, aluminium plates and screens with highly-polished surfaces, both Hara and Ito have been experimenting with innovative applications of glass to blur the differences between inside and out as well as between the real and the illusive, plus the rational and the intuitive. In this regard, Ito is now helped by the newly invented and now readily available 'electric' or liquid crystal glass that can render transparent surfaces partially or entirely opaque; it can act much like a film, yet the degree of change is controllable either manually or, through special monitors, by the intensity of the incoming sunshine, for example. Ito's competition entry for the planned Japanese Cultural Centre in Paris (1990) was based on the extensive use of this new technology, whose architectural potentials are expected to be far-reaching indeed.

Ito's architecture since the completion of his Silver Hut in 1984 has been consistently shaped in lightweight structures, ordinary and readily available industrial materials, unique and explicitly informal or 'no-form' compositions, and with new 'soft' technologies. By virtue of all these, his works have attained a 'primitive' simplicity, representing best what several other architects also pursue now, a new industrial vernacular.[30] His small residences and commercial facilities were meant to be temporary shelters for the members of a society increasingly comprised of 'urban nomads'.

This nomadic architecture, after the Silver Hut, has reached another milestone along the road; the Yatsushiro Municipal Museum (1991) is Ito's first really large-scale public building in which his new design paradigm has been brought to full maturity. An anti-monument by nature, the building, while redefining what we have hitherto understood as the essence of architecture, aspires to the ephemeral. This ephemerality, however, as Koji Taki explains, '(if) taken in a positive sense, never means that architecture is short-lived, but that new meanings are perpetually emerging'.[31] In such ephemerality, in conjunction with the perpetually emerging meanings, there emerges inevitably a *new space* as well. This space, figuratively speaking, does not exist *a priori*; it comes into being as a result of human actions, events and various phenomena occurring within and without. Space here not merely responds to, or receives and displays phenomena but, in a sense, it becomes the phenomena themselves; this is a space which is evoked as if by pantomime, and as such, it is both phenomenal and illusory.

Kazuyo Sejima's architecture, epitomised by her Platform Houses Nos I and 2 (1988 and 1990), has evolved precisely around this issue. She writes: 'Currently, my attempt is to make architecture overlap with actions that are performed discontinuously. When such momentary actions coincide with locales, a certain volume and detectable outline are derived. Another moment would bring a new outline. Thus a definitive, fixed image cannot proceed or emerge.'[32] The space that we encounter in the Platform No 2 or in Ito, Hara, and many others' buildings is thus not a

Hiromi Fujii, Mizoe 1, Iisuka

Hiromi Fujii, Mizoe 2

Fumihiko Maki, Metropolitan Gymnasium, Tokyo

Shin Takamatsu, Kirin Plaza Building, Osaka

real space; first, it is only an 'imminent space', and then, with action or events arising, it is an 'impromptu space', a space by performance.

It is important to emphasise again that the capability of circumventing the emergence of a definitive or 'consumable' image, in conjunction with forwarding a manifest critique of representation and/or the panoply of consumerist signs, is inseparably tied into promoting, if not provoking, human *action*, and therefore, the acquisition of a *knowledge* that goes far beyond the mere consumption of trivial and even high-tech spectacles. Yet such knowledge is not necessarily – or should not necessarily be – devoid of the power of dream. Many of these works appear indeed on the borderline between concrete reality and the freedom of dream, and thus in them Michel Foucault's excellent analysis finds itself carried on further while slightly readjusted.

Conclusion

Today, in the accelerated and simulated environment of Japan, as most of the examples discussed here seem to prove, a resistive practice in architecture tends to be implicated or absorbed to some extent in the very processes it intends to oppose or keep in check at least. Maintaining a critical position therefore may mean to pursue a practice which, while equally at odds with both technological domination and rampant consumerism together with its relentless drive for image making, acknowledges their *modus operandi* as the last viable alternative towards an architectural and perhaps also urban renewal.

This much is clear from the words of Toyo Ito, one of the most sensitive thinkers of his generation:

'. . . I believe architecture [today] must reflect the city called Tokyo. . . . [R]ight now [in the Japanese city] life and architecture itself are gradually losing their reality. They are not down-to-earth. I often use the word 'floating' not only to describe a lightness I want to achieve in architecture, but also to express a belief that our lives are losing touch with reality. All of life is becoming a pseudo-experience. This trend is being encouraged by the consumer society, and architecture itself is rapidly becoming more image-

or consumption-oriented. This is a matter of grave concern to the architect yet, at the same time, architecture today must be made to relate to this situation. This is the contradiction we are confronted with.'

And he goes on to say: 'I do not want merely to reject this state of affairs; instead, I want to enter into this situation a bit further and to confirm what sort of architecture is possible [within it].'[33]

Thus, in order to attempt to create a more meaningful relationship between reality and fiction many Japanese architects are taking upon the opponent, that is the simulated world of the city, on its own terms. This, however – as we have seen – is not without some serious risks of its own. The danger in such an 'undercover' operation is that, upon entering and sharing the 'reality' of the opponent, the hunter – as in Kobo Abe's novel *The Ruined Map* – can easily turn out to be or turn into the hunted itself.[34] Therefore, paradoxically again, to be able to shift toward another, more liberating reality, Japanese architects have to open an invisible gap between their architecture and the present, simulated and schizophrenic reality of society in the direction of the truly phenomenal and the ephemeral, and then see how far they can go without running into the ultimate paradox, that is the now very possible condition in which, in order to be saved, architecture has to be ultimately abandoned. To avoid such a pitfall, as Koji Taki pointed out, architects at the same time have to produce and maintain, even if 'a very slight, discrepancy, between architecture and the truly ephemeral'.[35]

This is a delicate and risky game, yet it is the only one that architects can and have to play today to keep alive any hope for the future. And what they need, in order to play successfully such a double role, is a high degree of critical self-awareness or a critical knowledge that can be disseminated through the gap their works open between their own reality of the 'truly' ephemeral and the simulated one at large. All this is necessary, because ours may be the dawn of a New Age, the age of a post-urban/post-ideal society, but it is certainly not a post-ideological one.

Notes

1 Michel Foucault, *Madness and Civilisation – A History of Insanity in the Age of Reason*, Richard Howard (trans), Vintage Books, New York, 1988 (1965), pp18-19.

2 The Crystal Light, Tarlazzi Building and the Nomad Restaurant were all featured in the previous special issue 'Japanese Architecture', *Architectural Design* Vol 58, No 5/6, 1988.

3 Data provided in *Corporate Design & Reality*, Oct 1985, special issue on 'Corporate Japan', p35.

4 Yutaka Hikosaka, 'Tokyo 1940-2000: The Death of the "City" and the End of "Theories of Tokyo"', *The Japan Architect*, 3/1991, pp10-11.

5 The Japanese often consider their traditionally small home with the elevated tatami flooring as a 'large bed': Shozaburo Kimura, *Kazoku no Jidai: Yoroppa to Nihon* (The Era of the Family: Europe and Japan), Shinchosha, Tokyo, 1985, p46.

6 Toyo Ito, 'Primitive Hut in the Modern City', *The Japan Architect*, May, 1985, p30.

7 Peter Eisenman is quoted in Kenneth Powell, 'Mapping the Modern', in 'Aspects of Modern Architecture', *Architectural Design*, Profile No 90, 1991, p7.

8 Rem Koolhaas, *Delirious New York: A Retroactive Manifesto for Manhattan*, New York and London, 1978.

9 Koji Taki, 'Towards an Open Text. On the Work and Thought of Toyo Ito', in S Roulet and S Soulie (eds), *Toyo Ito*, Editions du Moniteur, Paris, 1991, p12.

10 Japan expects a 3.5% GNP increase in 1992 relative to the previous 6%.

11 Peter Cook in an interview on the occasion of his appointment as a professor at Bartlett School of Architecture, London University, *Building Design*, 5 Jan, 1990.

12 Among the three, Le Corbusier was the most influential, while the impact of Wright and Raymond, despite their longer affiliation with Japan, was much less. For further details see David B Stewart, *The Making of a Modern Architecture: 1868*

to the Present, Kodansha International, Tokyo and New York, 1987.

13 Fumihiko Maki, 'Driving Force of the 1990s', *The Japan Architect*, 2/1991, p7.

14 Hajime Yatsuka, 'Between Reality and Unreality', *The Japan Architect*, 4/1991, p10.

15 H Yatsuka, 'Arata Isozaki after 1980: From Mannerism to the Picturesque', in *Arata Isozaki: Architecture 1960-1990*, Rizzoli, New York, p19.

16 Parts of the argument on Shin Takamatsu's work is based on Botond Bognar, 'Monuments in Search of Meaning – The Work of Shin Takamatsu', in *The Japan Architect,* extra edition on Shin Takamatsu, 1992 (forthcoming).

17 H Yatsuka, *op cit* 15, p23.

18 Takefumi Aida in the 1970s referred to his work as an architecture of 'silence'; some of his buildings were covered with earth at that time. In the case of Takamatsu, this statement refers to only some of his recent works such as the Sunset Cathedral.

19 Riken Yamamoto, 'The City as Topography', *The Japan Architect*, Nov/Dec, 1986, p42.

20 Itsuko Hasegawa, 'Architecture as Another Nature & Recent Projects', in 'Aspects of Modern Architecture', *Architectural Design,* profile No 90, p14.

21 See Kitagawara's comments in his project descriptions in this issue.

22 It is important to point out that the circular elements along which the Temple's plan was constructed can be read as the signs of Zen Buddhism, insofar as the circle or *enso* in Zen expressed enlightenment and oneness with nature.

23 For further details on the new technology in Japan see B Bognar, 'Architecture, Nature & A New Technological Landscape', in 'Aspects of Modern Architecture', *Architectural Design*, Profile No 90, p32.

24 T Aida, 'From Toy-Blocks to an Architecture of Fluctuation', *Shinkenchiku*, June, 1987, p203.

25 Hiromi Fujii, 'Ushimado International Arts Festival Centre' in 'Japanese Architecture', *Architectural Design,* Vol 58, No 5/6, 1988, p48.

26 Details from a conversation of the author with F Maki in July 1991, also described in Sally Woodbridge, 'Foreword: How Amazing Buildings are Made in Japan', in Hiroshi Watanabe, *Amazing Architecture from Japan*, Weatherhill, Tokyo and New York, p7.

27 B Bognar, *op cit* 16.

28 The media show in the Museum of Phenomenart was actually Yoh's own idea and design, just as much as the system of light towers on the Kirin Building was Takamatsu's.

29 I Hasegawa, 'Urbanism and the Poetic Machine', *Space Design*, 04/1985, p55.

30 T Ito, *op cit.*

31 K Taki, *op cit*, p17.

32 Kazuyo Sejima, 'Platform No 1' in B Bognar, *The New Japanese Architecture*, Rizzoli, New York , 1990, p221.

33 T Ito, 'Shinjuku Simulated City', *The Japan Architect* 3/1991, p51.

34 Kobo Abe, *The Ruined Map*, Dale Saunders (trans), Tuttle, Tokyo, 1970.

35 T Taki, *op cit*, p17.

Toyo Ito, 'Tower of the Wind', Yokohama

Yasumitsu Matsunaga, Forest Green Housing, Tokyo

Shin Takamatsu, Kunibiki Messe, cross section through the 'Garden of Abstract Forms'

TOYO ITO
VORTEX AND CURRENT
On Architecture as Phenomenalism

The scene of a cherry-blossom viewing party, where people drink sake with friends on a red carpet under the trees and paper lanterns, or inside open tents, represents the fundamental character of Japanese architecture.

First of all, people come together to see the cherry blossoms in full bloom, and then primitive architecture (ie, the carpet and the tent) is built for the event. It is not that the architecture is there at the beginning; on the contrary, it is the human act of getting together that exists first. It is only afterwards that architecture comes into being to envelope this action.

Such architecture does not confront, but assimilates nature completely. This is because the presence of cherry trees alone is capable of creating a unique space; with petals dancing in the wind, the beauty of the scene is visually enhanced. As carpets are spread on suitable ground, and tents are stretched, taking into account the favourable wind and sunshine conditions, architecture is installed as a minimal filter to visualise natural phenomena rather than disregard or suppress them. Cherry trees stretch their branches above the tents, petals incessantly fall on people who fully enjoy the pleasant scene within nature.

The party reaches its peak when at sunset dusk deepens and the scene is veiled in increasing darkness. Some start singing while others dance to the music. As the night wears on, the people, getting tired of pleasure, take down the tents and go home, leaving the cherry blossom floating in the dark like white clouds. The end of the event means the simultaneous end of the architecture as well.

It may be said that the architecture here is evoked by something extremely transient; like a piece of film wrapping the human body, it does not have much substance nor does it imply significant weight.

Designing architecture is an act of generating vortexes in the currents of air, wind, light, and sound; it is not constructing a dam against the flow nor resigning itself to the current. For instance, if a pole is erected in the river, changes are caused in the current around the pole. If two poles are placed at a short distance from each other, the movement of water changes complicatedly due to their synergetic effect.

In nature, the place where people choose to gather is determined by the terrain, the location of the trees, or the direction of the wind. If the gathering place is in an urban setting, it is also selected by other considerations: the relationship among buildings, the flow of transportation and communication and the information exchange among all the constituents. In both natural and urban settings, however, when architectural elements such as posts and screens are placed within space, the natural currents – the flow of wind, sound, information, transportation, etc –

change, instantly causing small eddies around the installations. A vortex like this could be regarded as a minimal device to create a place for the gathering of people. In order to turn such a gesture into an architectural act, it is necessary to organise these architectural elements into an entity. The organisation may be a kind of structure or style in an abstract sense. When given a certain form, the place for an event becomes architecture. This is done so that the flow of phenomena will not end as merely a passing one, but is to be perpetuated while incorporated into a more stable and orderly system.

When architecture is defined according to the concept outlined above, people can remain within the surrounding currents of nature and/or the city, while at the same time situated in a framework of architectural form; they are enveloped simultaneously in two contradictory spaces: in an unstable, ephemeral phenomenon, as well as in a system which constantly seeks stability and continuity. Architecture today is bound to have a precarious existence; it has to keep a delicate balance in an ambiguous and unstable space, insofar as there is no longer a solid foundation on which architecture can stand firmly. Architecture seeking a passing phenomenon alone and resigning itself to the present with no resistance, will be immediately and completely consumed. Conversely, a piece of architecture which is anachronistically monumental, relying on a style that is no more than a cliché, would not attain empathy in our contemporary dynamic world.

A more appropriate act of architecture may be analogous to the linguistic art which extracts words as symbols from the fleeting feeling of an individual, gives them a style, and organises them. Vivid verbal expressions can be created only from the confrontation of a style with a direction while deviating from it to voice individual emotion. The same is applicable to architecture.

To give life today to architecture and let it breathe, it is vital to constantly generate vortexes of events and currents connecting these vortexes against the movement of formalisation which always seeks a rigidly fixed and stable order. It is critical to aim at spaces of unstable states which may be conducive to a movement or flow. Such spaces are also analogous to the physical movement of humans. In *Noh*, one of the traditional stage arts of Japan, comparable to *Kabuki*, the posture of the actor reveals a certain anxiety as his sight is extremely limited by his mask. His torso is inclined forwards and then lifted upwards throwing out his chest. Only when the actor assumes this posture can he attain a counter-force against the anxiety. Noh-dance is not a mere walk on the stage but a movement induced by the force drawn from inside the body. As Keiichiro Tsuchiya described, Noh-dance becomes a dynamic fluid and, as the actor undergoes a passive experience by wearing his mask, restructures the whole space of the stage.

According to a master of *kendo*, the basic technique of this martial art lies in the use of instability. More precisely, in kendo an unstable posture of standing on two feet is seen as an advantage rather than as a deficiency. Therefore, students are trained to move both feet simultaneously to remove the fulcrum of the body.

Just as the human body, supported by a stable structure, can generate force or movement only when in an unstable state, architecture also needs to create a flow of space against stability while constantly seeking stable forms.

The act of creating, or rather, choreographing a piece of architecture in a city like Tokyo is akin to playing chess. It is a completely unpredictable game. Buildings all around a particular construction site differ in volume, form, height,

material and structure. Moreover, there is no way of knowing when these buildings will be demolished and replaced by something else. And this is also an endless game. What then is the context we can consider or hope for against such a fleeting urban scene as background?

In a chessboard-like urban space such as ours, what we can achieve with any of our next moves is merely to create a temporary, tense relationship. In other words, what we can do is simply to throw in a new vortex to stir or stimulate the space and to induce a new flow.

A new vortex is like a tent for the improvised theatre on a vacant lot. We don't need any other forms of architecture apart from those which, like video images, appear for an event and disappear when the event ends. Tokyo no longer requires the lasting stability of formalistic expressions, let alone the permanence of monuments.

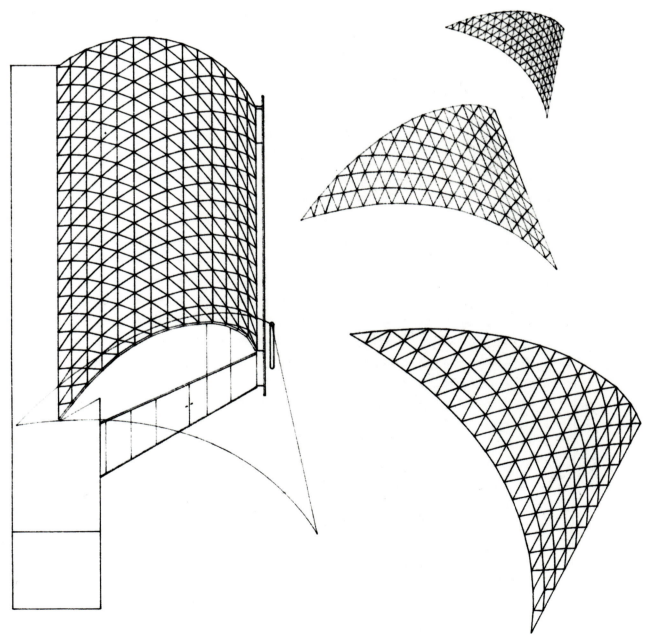

LEFT & ABOVE: Toyo Ito, Ueda Gallery, Yugawara

VLADIMIR KRSTIC
STILLNESS OF HYPERREALITY
The In(de)finite City

Shinjuku district, Tokyo

The reason for the visual chaos and physical impermanence of the Japanese metropolis have been repeatedly
sought in the idea of destruction as a major force through
which the city and its understanding have been shaped.
Japanese architectural historian Riichi Miyake clearly
articulated this idea by stating:

> . . . that the historical growth of certain Japanese
> cities has not been a continuous flow and that it has
> been always motivated by some catastrophic event.
> The will to build a city and to construct a building
> has been constantly next to the reality of destruction
> and included an impulse to destroy the unified
> whole. [1]

Although such insights embody a profound grasp of the
particular urban condition, it is necessary to move beyond
their generalising framework in order to recognise the
archetypal destructive event that constitutes the inerasable,
physical and conceptual origin of the Japanese contemporary city: the destruction of castle towns. The Meiji
Reformation of 1867 resulted not only in profound socio-
cultural transformations in Japan but also in massive and
violent physical changes of its major cities. The collapse of
the entire socio-political system rendered the correspond-
ing iconographic idea of city – the castle town – void. Now
emptied of its political content, a condition graphically
signified by the literal destruction and vacation of the
castle as its topological and symbolic centre, the spatial
order of the town was deprived of any further authority to
subordinate and relate. The consequent reduction of the
city to a system of abstract physical properties and
relationships opened it up to commercial exploitation by
the freed powers of capital which were solely concerned
with the pragmatic opportunism of new urban circumstances devoid of any conscious desire to articulate a
specific idea of urbanity. [2]

The two extreme aspects of this situation – the destruction of the urban model that embodied the idea of totality,
and the emergence of the non-ideological, fragmentary
vision of the city framed by the autonomy of capitalist
pragmatism – denote the point of origin of the modern
Japanese city. Accordingly, it can be argued that the
modern 'decentred' Japanese city has developed with no
apparent concept of a larger totality. Signifying the tri-
umph of what Tafuri called a 'will to formlessness', the
constituting urban parts have achieved utmost autonomy
while engaging the city in the perpetuation of random
relationships. [3]

The most important aspect of the chaotic urban condition brought about by the uncontrollable proliferation of
autonomous parts, is the displacement and subversion of
any fixed sense of reality. The primary reason for this
phenomenon resides in the obliteration of an idea(l) city
plan whose uprooting has eliminated the existence and
authority of an external 'referent' against which the reality
of the built environment could be measured. The modern
Japanese city hence embodies an inverse (or antithetical)
concept of urbanity where individual urban artefacts
invent and frame their own realities; they are independent
of each other and the city as a whole which, within this
process, comes to represent an elusive, almost non-
physical form of a locale. Created through such haphaz-
ard constructions, the hybrid structure of the city envelops
its own territory with an incessant spectacle of urban
phantasmagory in which delirious acts of architecture
stand in indifferent juxtaposition to engineering stunts and
to the perverse contraptions of electronic technology. The
city thus appears as a surreal, panoptic vision composed
of virtually impossible and mutually cancelling physical
and temporal perspectives. The disappearance of the
idea(l) framework of references has reduced the production of the city to a self-referential activity where the idea of
reality has no particular relevance; while its parameters
remain in the continuous flux perpetuated by the ideologi-
cally unbounded production process itself, reality can only
be circumstantially and temporarily inscribed in the city.

The physical and cultural pervasiveness of the Japanese city circumscribes the inescapable locus of architecture where the validity of all modes of architectural
production can only be measured against one single
parameter: the schizophrenic texture of the city. While in
the West the 'problem' of city is largely a theoretical
construct that reads and interprets the city in excess of its
physical condition, in Japan the dynamism of commercial
distribution and consumption process – whose instrument
and ultimate object being the urban environment itself –
physically transforms the city at a rate that surpasses the
most imaginative theoretical speculation. The city, engen-
dered through such processes in the weightlessness of a
confining ideological vacuum, constitutes a physical entity
whose configuration and meaning cannot be accounted
through any given set of conceptual precepts. Hence
architecture is confronted with the city as an unintelligible
and chaotic object. Since the actualisation of architecture
is contingent upon discovering the parameters of its own
reality in a particular locus, this object must be interpreted
and articulated as a theoretical proposition, through the
working of architecture's *own* spatial and formal structures. Every act of architecture is thus founded in the need
to construct a hypothetical resolution of the city as a basis
for the argumentation and assertion of its own authenticity.
Conceived and applied in such a way, architecture as a
sum of practical acts constitutes an experimental (and

apparently only viable) tool of inquiry into the condition of the city where conceptual insights and concrete actions are synonymous and derived through the direct encounter with the chaotic urban matter.

The paradox of this situation lies in the fact that the eventual resolution of the city can never happen within a work of architecture itself. Given the mechanisms that generate its hybrid structure, the city possesses no subsumable reality and hence remains opposed to and infinitely outside of architecture's capacity to rationalise its objects. As Koji Taki points out: 'In the Japanese city, architecture is not symbolic of the city as a whole; it can never be more than partial or fragmentary.'[4] This contention could be taken to imply two critical points. First, it denotes the fact that architecture has lost the capacity to maintain its own autonomy with the dissolution of all attempts to revise the chaos of the Japanese city according to the Modernist ideal of rationality. Second, it suggests that, since there is no fixed reality to the city, architecture can only be actualised as a fragment of its hybrid body in which case the city conversely symbolises architecture and delimits its capacity to signify. By the same analogy then the actual purpose of the desire to resolve the city within architecture can only be a resolution of architecture itself. If architecture is to sustain any relevance within the irreversible schizophrenia of the Japanese city, then the conventional (Modernist) means and concepts through which architecture constructs its own reality – and which are now rendered obsolete and ineffectual by the chaotic urban texture – must be revised and defined anew in its every act in order to maintain a critical engagement with the imposing uncertainty of the external world.

Fredric Jameson argues that in our Post-Modern culture we inhabit the space of 'perpetual present' analogous to the condition of schizophrenia where the inability of temporal conceptualisation of language reduces experience of the external world to the succession of disconnected and discontinuous moments: 'material signifiers'.[5] The consequent loss of correspondence between signifier and signified, a mental condition whose cultural equivalent Jameson sees in the failure of Post-Modern society to retain the past and focus the present, transforms the isolated signifier into an image whereby its meaning is lost and superseded by the intensified experience of its materiality. This eventually leads to the transformation of reality itself into an image.

This argument curiously echoes the condition of the Japanese city where the displacement of a sense of history, or any other temporal determinant, is induced by the perplexing syntax of urban fabric which comprises an infinite array of incoherent formal and physical elements. The schizophrenia of the Japanese city originates in the extreme process of commodification of the urban space in which the mechanisms of commercial distribution and consumption enact a manipulative subversion of real measurements of space and time through the eclecticism of the advertising process. Since the physical reality of the city within such a process is reduced to the function of commercial exchange, the city itself is realised as a fictitious construct whose realities are invented and manipulated by the advertising operations. The fictitiousness

of the city is constructed through the process analogous to the described transformative reduction of reality into images which, as an instrument of commercial advertising mechanisms, conceives and produces the urban environment as a collage of contrived eclectic scenes. The reality of these scenes, independent of and disinterested in the original situations and their circumstances, is authenticated by the materialisation of abstracted (architectural) forms. This marks the final point in the reduction of reality, a reality which, confined to a single image, acquires the status of replicable commodity.

The reduction of reality to images brings the chronological progression of time to a perceptual rest. The city, in spite of its perpetual turmoil, unfolds a paradoxical stillness that comprises the multitude of isolated and fragmented scenes; imbued with the surreal emptiness of the collapsed time found in still photos, such scenes fail to connect and generate the difference between relative temporal positions. The city appears transfixed in the ahistorical dimension of its composite body. It is constantly re-created, or made anew through the construction of new scenes and the dismantling of existing ones which, after having exhausted their commercial purpose, are removed without a trace thereby revealing in the moment of their own disappearance the actual structure of the city: the infinite void of oblivion. Hence, the visual noise of the Japanese city, termed by Kazuo Shinohara as the 'metropolis of no-memory', resonates with the amnesic silence of the 'perpetual present' where no fundamental change seems possible.[6]

However, what represents the unresolvable enigma of architectural theory and practice in the Japanese city, and what in a way has eliminated the possibility of the Modernist urban revision, is the fact that the very fictitiousness of the Japanese city constitutes the undeniable form of reality or, more precisely, the *city is rendered as its own fiction*, therefore reality can only be determined within the confines of that fiction.

As previously proposed, the texture of the Japanese city is constructed through images which denote reality as the materialisation of form and, to paraphrase Jean Baudrillard, these images substitute the real itself with signs of the real.[7] More importantly, having had their reference to original realities (objects and situations) abstracted through the eclectic structure of the urban context, these signs constitute 'models of (the) real without (the) origin of reality', hence they are 'hyperreal'.[8] The city therefore constitutes an absolute space of simulations imbued with the perverse vitality of impossible phenomena in perpetual unfolding which, generated through the hyperreal existence of urban artefacts, diffract space and time into the depthlessness of two-dimensionality. The materialisation of the city thus reflects a screen-like condition, where all projected phenomena are automatically inserted into a mesmerising realm. In this realm the real and the unreal appear as equidistant and synonymously interchangeable parameters that determine the existence of all things. Such volatility eliminates the possibility of discriminating between a metaphorical scene and real scene, between dream and its fulfilment, or more precisely, this discrimination is short-circuited by the infinitely simulative mode of

Toyo Ito, T-Building, Nakameguro

25

Hiroshi Hara, Iida City Museum

the Japanese city where all things share the same hyperreal appearance.

Reality has been reduced to materialised form which can be replicated through the hyperreal objects (urban artefacts), the question of the physical veracity of those objects appears as an inevitable and critical issue. The fact that the image itself is reality implies that the act of (re)tracing its form fulfils the requirement for the production of reality. As there are no other contingencies of reality, the progression of the initial reductive process is carried into infinity whereby the original object is physically abstracted into a mask, a dematerialised membrane, or eventually a TV screen. The disconnection between the city as a hyperreal, simulated object and its physical body thus becomes imminent. With its reality embedded in the dematerialised images that float in space, the structure of the city that underlies those images appears anonymous and obsolete as an 'archaic envelope'.[9]

In the Japanese city the fundamental problem of architecture resides not only in the fact that its production has become debased by the elimination of reality itself as a field of reference in which all of its premises and actions are grounded but also, even more importantly, in the fact that the very concept of architecture's corporeality has been called to question. The relegation of meaning (reality) into an autonomous system of two-dimensional codes has delineated the antithetical and annihilating counterpoint to the concept of architecture as a vessel which, in its physical, spatial and formal relationships, contains instances of an undeniable reality. Hence what once was considered real now seems to be void or, as Baudrillard has phrased it, 'The real itself appears as a large useless body' that marks the pending eclipse of architecture.[10]

So, what are the perspectives left when the entire foundation on which architecture can be thought of and acted upon appears to be irreversibly undermined? In the enormous output of explorative designs by contemporary Japanese architects two positions of ideological extremes can be identified. One position, held by architects like Tadao Ando, is marked by the adherence to the Modernist concept of architectural autonomy, and is used as a form of critique and eventual rejection of the city. The other position, whose proponents are architects like Shin Takamatsu and Atsushi Kitagawara, suggests their acceptance of the existing condition of the city as an inescapable and unresolvable destiny of architecture; this position is subsequently used as a pretext for the indulgence and the legitimisation of the most decadent and inaccessibly personal architectural travesties.

Both of these positions, along with the others in between, appear equally hopeless relative to the resolution of urban impasse of architecture. Their hopelessness resides in the continuing desire to engage architecture as an object; a proposition which remains blind to the fact of its own impossibility circumscribed by the loss of the meaning of corporeality of architecture in the Japanese city. These positions, seeing the city solely in terms of architecture's 'archaic' parameters, are consequently incapable of truly constructive confrontation with its hyperreality which must be encountered through its own annihilating mechanisms if the conceptual recovery of architecture is to be made possible. Only by recognising the hyperreality of the city as a zero degree condition of architecture from where all attempts for its (re)construction and (re)discovery have to start can there be a chance for a genuine exploration, otherwise all architectural production remains mere proliferation of consumable images.

In this respect the work of Hiroshi Hara and Toyo Ito appears particularly significant. Although they do not necessarily share identical ideological and/or theoretical positions, their works bear resemblance relative to their focusing on the problematic reality of architecture. They both recognise that the problematic of reality stems not only from the compromised proposition of the idea of corporeality, but also from the fact that what architecture is to enclose and contain as a corporeal thing has equally become compromised. Since reality as a sum of rational measurements and parameters has become an unsustainable concept, each of these designers in his own way has forwarded architecture along the desire to dismantle whatever is left of the pretence of reality, implicitly arguing that the reality of architecture in the context of the Japanese city is that there is no reality. In their work, architecture is proposed as a field of exploration of untold and unforeseen dimensions found in the experiential and imaginative limitlessness of time, space and matter. This shift in focus seems to tend towards the dismantling of the opacity of architecture's boundaries and towards eventually transforming it into a transparent locus – as opposed to an object – where events unfold in a phantasmagorical way with no sense of temporal or physical limit. The only certainty (reality) that constitutes such an architecture is found in the experience of the *event* itself which is bounded by the ephemeral immeasurability of an instant. Simultaneously the whole idea of corporeality appears redefined in a fascinating way when the intensity of architecture's material existence is achieved in the moment of its physical abstraction and pending disappearance with the purpose not to concretise the object itself but create a perceptual mirage.

This tenuous line that separates existence from non-existence, along which Hara and Ito's work unfolds, seems to denote a subversive twist of the simulative hyperreality of the city which, within the hopeless stillness of its world, promises to open up to an entirely new realm of phenomenal and existential dimensions of architecture and in which the mythical poiesis of building appears as a not yet extinct possibility. Yet, their work can still be criticised as much as the activity of the 17th-century *sukiya* masters for example, who were accused of overindulgence in the aesthetic matters of architecture as a form of political escapism. However, if the alternative to their architecture, relative to the problematic of the Japanese city, is a looming corporate totalitarianism as evidenced by projects like Kenzo Tange's new Tokyo City Hall complex, then not only does the choice become self-evident, but at the same time the work of Hara and Ito attains an important political perspective.

Notes

1 Riichi Miyake, 'Pursuit for Internal Microcosms', *The Japan Architect*, January 1987, p6.
2 For further discussion of these issues see John W Hall, 'The Castle Town and Japan's Modern Urbanisation', *Far Eastern Quarterly* Vol XV, No I, November 1955; Ken-ichi Tanabe, 'Intraregional Structure of Japanese Cities', in *Japanese Cities: A Geographical Approach*, Association of Japanese Geographers, Tokyo, 1970; Takeo Yazaki, *Historical Geography of Urban Morphology*, Tameiro, Tokyo, 1970.
3 Manfredo Tafuri, *Architecture and Utopia*, MIT Press, Cambridge, Mass, 1988, p16.
4 Koji Taki, 'Fragments and Noise', *Architectural Design*, Vol 58, 5/6, 1988, p34.
5 Fredric Jameson, 'Postmodernism and Consumer Society', in Hal Foster, (ed) *The Anti-Aesthetic*, Bay Press, Port Townsend, Wash, 1983.
6 Kazuo Shinohara, 'The Context of Pleasure', *The Japan Architect*, September 1986, p23.
7 Jean Baudrillard, 'The Precession of Simulacra', in Brian Wallis, (ed) *Art After Modernism: Rethinking Representation*, MOCA, New York, 1984, p254.
8 *Ibid*, p253.
9 Jean Baudrillard, 'The Ecstasy of Communication', in Hal Foster, (ed) The *Anti-Aesthetic*, Bay Press, Port Townsend, Wash, 1986, p129.
10 *Ibid*, p129.

Shinjuku district, Tokyo

ARATA ISOZAKI
ART TOWER, MITO

This cultural complex occupies a block in the old part of Mito. More than half of the site is given over to an urban square around which the facility itself is designed as a small townscape. This square or plaza is accessible from four directions and is open to the public day and night. The cultural centre commemorates Mito's centenary with a 100-metre-high symbolic tower, incorporating a theatre, a concert hall, and a gallery of contemporary art. Although activities are accommodated in separate facilities, the spaces are close to one another and have a common area so that interrelationships can develop across different fields. The theatre and the concert hall are located along the western street, and between them is the entrance hall for the entire complex, which is equipped with a pipe organ. On the northern street, behind a cascade on the square, are offices, curatorial rooms, a restaurant on the first floor, and the gallery on the second. A two-storey

conference hall is located on the southwestern corner of the square. Underground facilities include rehearsal and dressing rooms, art-storage space and a car park.

With a composition based on that of Shakespeare's Globe, the theatre has a cylindrical, interior brick wall into which are inserted the wooden structures of three balconies. The concert hall seats 700 and is small, in an arena style with a hexagonal floor plan. Its circular ceiling is supported by an arch and three columns. Each of the continuous series of seven exhibition rooms in the modern art gallery are varied by means of spatial volume and lighting conditions. The tower with titanium covering symbolises the entire complex. With a twisted triple spiral configuration, it is made up of regular quadrilaterals. The kind of symbolism that was carefully avoided in the case of the Tsukuba Centre Building is employed in this case to make the Mito Museum of Art a monument to the whole city.

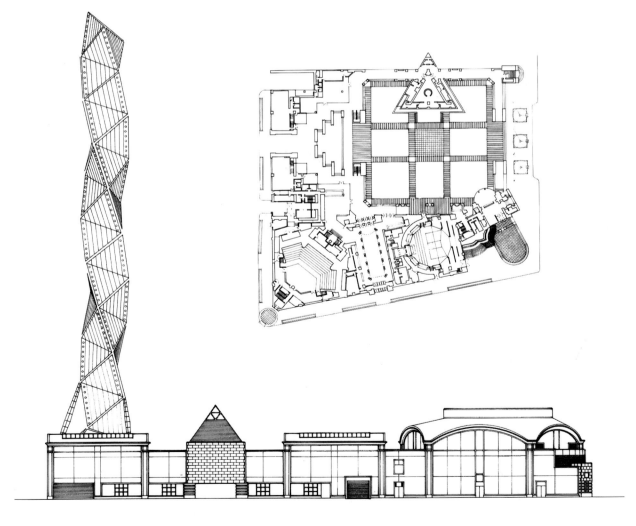

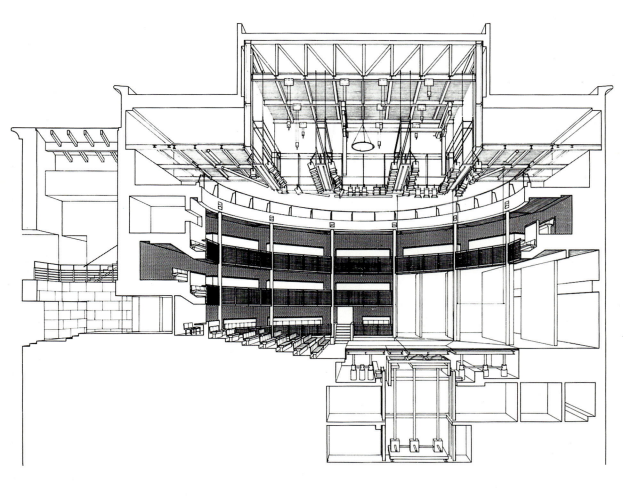

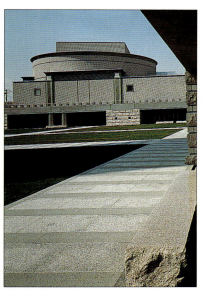

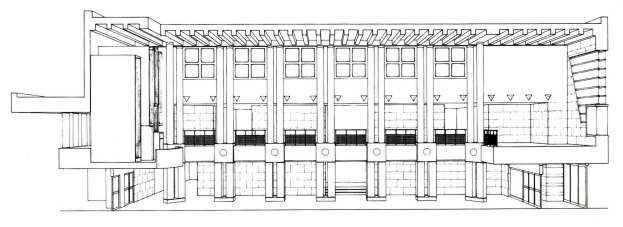

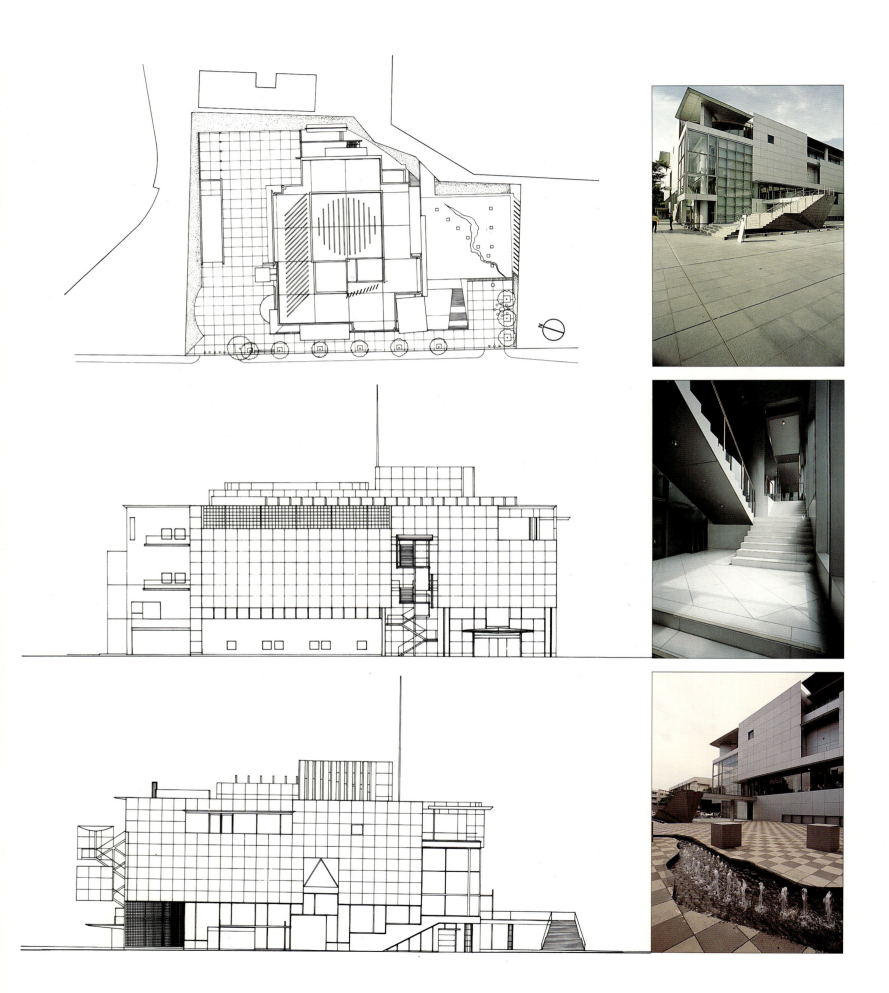

FUMIHIKO MAKI
TEPIA BUILDING, TOKYO

Tepia, a pavilion for science and high-technology is located in Meiji Memorial Park, not far from the centre of Tokyo. The building appears to be a free-standing pavilion surrounded by open space, as it takes advantage of the zoning regulations of the Park District which delimits the volume and height of the building above ground. An organisation affiliated to the Ministry of International Trade and Industry is the owner of Tepia and is entrusted to offer a place to exhibit the most advanced products of high-technology and electronics – robots, computers, computer arts, etc. The building and its exhibits are intended to provide an exchange of recent knowledge and information among professionals and the public.

The building consists of four floors above ground and two floors below. On the ground floor, there are three different spaces in sequence, each designated to offer various kinds of exhibitions organised by Tepia. A video library, small lecture room and café are located on the second floor, easily accessible from the ground floor by a screened stairway and bridge. The facilities on the second floor can also be approached directly from the street via a large stair which floats upon a reflecting pool. The third floor accommodates a large rentable exhibition space which may be divided by sliding partitions. A conference hall with a capacity of 200 people, seminar rooms, and a membership club, are all organised around a courtyard on the top floor. In the two floors below ground, is a restaurant, sports club, and parking garage.

The design principles and aesthetics of Tepia in both the exterior and interior are intended to reflect the character and spirit of our time as well as communicating the requirements of the programme. A composition of primary elements of planes and lines were put to force, and where the planes and lines meet one another, is the creation of a 'point', the third primary element in the composition. The distinctive skyline of Tepia is born through the combination of vertical walls and horizontal overhangs and, at the point at which they intersect, a tight gap is revealed to heighten the tension of collision and separation. In the interior stairway, perforated panels of aluminium are suspended in the air by cables, leaving lines of light between the panels. The means to express the energy embodied in the 'points' both compositionally and materially has been investigated and exercised from the largest scale of the building to the smallest of details.

Such compositions of planes, lines, and points, are best achieved with the use of metals and glass which are primary materials of modern architecture; however, new means of mobilising these materials in the exterior aluminium panels, structural glass, and solar-air panels of aluminium extrusions on the roof, which are the latest industrially produced products of building technology, express our own time, in which the building is realised.

In an effort to avoid the monolithic repetitious uses of the same materials, finishes, and details, Tepia attempts to introduce a variety of these to create a subtle yet sumptuous ambience. This strategy has been employed throughout all the rooms, ramp-ways, corridors, stairways, and even the mechanical spaces, to achieve the overall quality unique to this building. The same principles have been applied in the colour co-ordination where white, grey, silver and black and their rich combinations comprise the spectrum. The principle is intentionally interrupted in some locations in order to amplify the effect – for instance, red in the carpet of the lounge, green in the courtyard, and brown paint on the walls.

The high standard of technology and craftsmanship maintained by Japan's system of building and construction has made this design and its details possible. In all likelihood, an equivalent level of technology and craftsmanship may not endure indefinitely. Thus Tepia, in a sense, is a testimony to Japanese society of today.

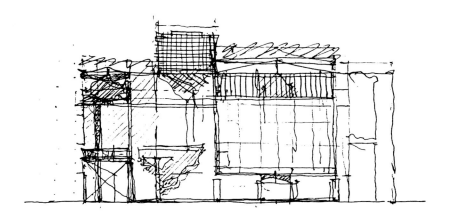

TOKYO METROPOLITAN GYMNASIUM

The Tokyo Metropolitan Gymnasium is a reconstruction of the old facility built 30 years ago which was quite inadequate and poorly constructed. The new Gymnasium, designed under a new programme of a total floor area of 45,000 square metres was constructed on the same site of four hectares. The programme consists of a much larger main arena with a seating capacity of 10,000, compared to the original 6,000, an indoor swimming pool with a 50-metre pool with less spectator seating, more backup facilities, and an additional 25-metre training pool. Additions included in the new programme are a sub-arena, primarily used as a practice gym, training courts, meeting rooms for sports seminars, sports exhibition, generously appropriated administration spaces, and a restaurant. This sports complex, revitalised in its original form, is open to all citizens and serves as a stage for both international and national indoor sporting events.

The grounds for the Tokyo Metropolitan Gymnasium are part of the larger Meiji Park with Sendagaya Station to the north, residential and commercial complexes to the south and west, and the National Stadium to the east beyond a boulevard that drops lower than the site. While it is quite rare to find such a large parcel of open land in the densely built Tokyo, the entire site is treated as an urban park that is open at all hours. Sendagaya Station, the gateway for most visitors to the sports park, becomes a pivotal point for access to the main arena, the glass pyramidal visitors' entrance, the swimming pool, and to the stairway leading to the deck serving as a public thoroughfare through the site. The paths, proceeding to each, disperse radially from the Station, forming diagonal vistas and movements on arrival.

The height restriction imposed on the site of a maximum of 30 metres, necessitated to lower the main arena floor six metres below ground level and the swimming pool two metres below. The design, conforming to the height restrictions, avoids the appearance of the massive and voluminous spaces of the required interiors and harmonises as a friendly neighbour to the residential and commercial buildings in proximity. While the volumes of the respective buildings in the complex are constrained to be quite low, the roof shapes for each building is given a significant architectonic role – a continuous investigation of Fujisawa Municipal Gymnasium (1984) and Makuhari Messe (1989). The roof of the main arena gently curving as in a shell, the sub-arena stepping as in a ziggurat, the undulating roof and hovering eaves of the swimming pool, the transparent pyramid, together with the sculptures and red lighting fixtures constitute a new urban-scape. While moving through the sports park, visitors will always be faced with changing views due to the different juxtapositions of the buildings with different vistas of the neighbouring park and city. The experience of changing sceneries is not unlike that of the Japanese *kaiyushiki* or stroll garden.

While the main arena, sub-arena, and indoor swimming pool possess independence through their distinct size, shape, and form, they have been dynamically knit together through the use of materials – primarily of metal, glass, and concrete. In mobilising these materials, much attention has been paid to the details throughout, giving the materials energy and vitality.

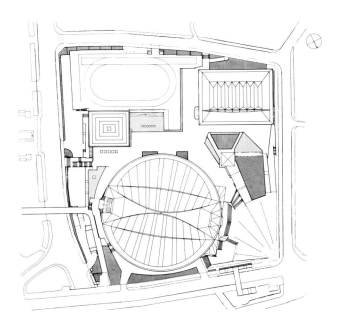

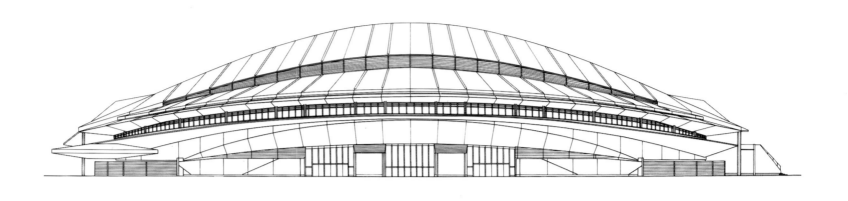

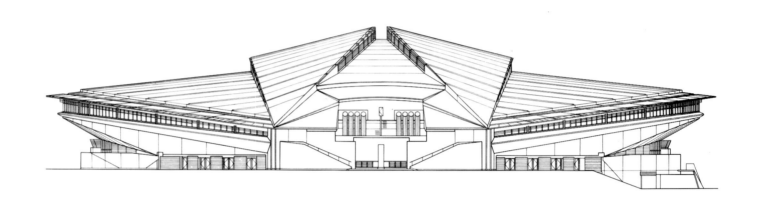

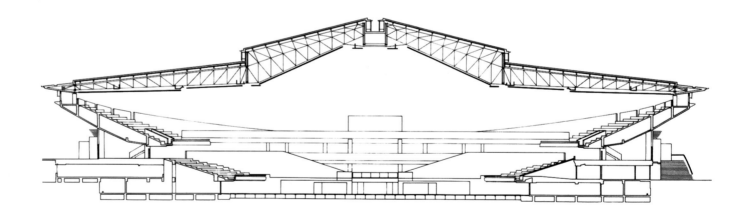

FROM ABOVE: ELEVATION, CROSS AND LONGITUDINAL SECTIONS OF MAIN ARENA, AND ELEVATION OF SWIMMING POOL

KISHO KUROKAWA
OKINAWA PREFECTURAL GOVERNMENT HEADQUARTERS, NAHA

The layout of the New Okinawa Government Headquarters, which is a huge complex of the governmental administration offices, parliament, and police headquarters, has been designed to maintain the optimum use of the existing buildings on the site during construction of the new complex. In order to fit in with the overall context of the Naha cityscape the whole site is landscaped, utilising a harmonious combination of straight and curved lines, and retaining the affluent greenery existing in the area. Also, a central courtyard is provided in each building in order to promote natural lighting and ventilation in the tropical climate.

Distinctively different materials, including stone, terrazzo, tiles, aluminium and titanium are introduced for the facade as if woven textiles to express the symbiosis of tradition and future. The silhouette of the roof is the metaphoric introduction of the roof of traditional village houses.

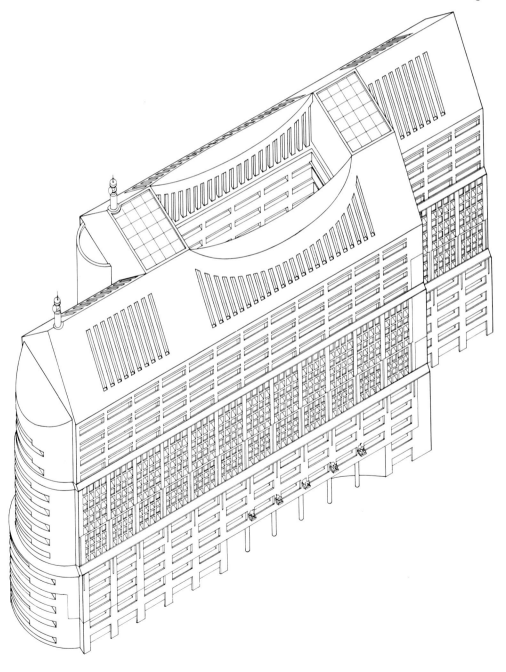

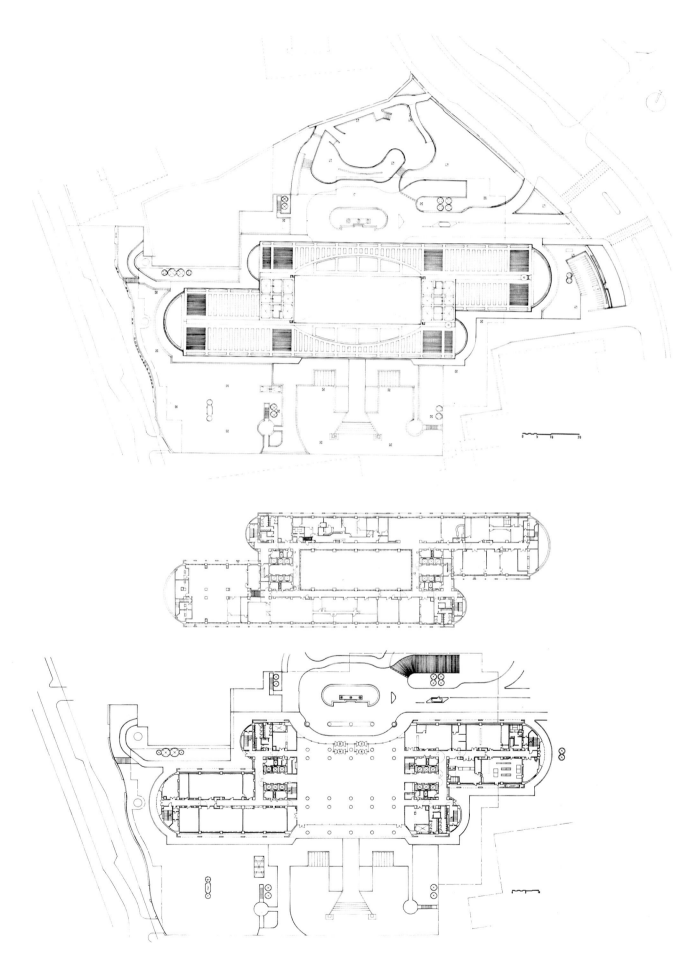

ABOVE, CENTRE & BELOW: ROOF, 13TH-FLOOR AND GROUND FLOOR PLANS

41

KAZUO SHINOHARA
K-2 BUILDING, OSAKA

Kyobashi Station, the junction point between the Osaka Loop Line and the Keihan Electric Railway, is 90 metres southeast of the site. Restrictions were placed on the amount of load that can rest on the northwest corner of the site, where the subway passes along a slanting line.

The main theme of the project was to differentiate between the expressions of the north and south elevations but to achieve this, not as a result of superficial ornamentation, but structurally by 'connecting [these] heterogeneous framework systems'.

A parking tower for 30 cars is positioned within the framework on the north side. Its exterior finish is white aluminium panels. The third-storey level, which, finished with the same panels, resembles a composite drawing and houses an event hall to be used mainly for exhibitions. The catwalk suspended in the sixth-storey level of the wide space on top of the hall is a major architectural feature.

On the west side, where it was necessary to abide by load limitations and to avoid the subway tubes, I have provided an added composition with a two-level space on the third storey and a one-level space on the seventh storey. This embodies the basic plan concept of ensuring that the elevations occupy maximum frontage adjacent to the roads.

Several kinds of glass have been employed in different elevations. The north elevation uses transparent glass, but the added composition on the west is half-mirror glass. On the south, braces demarcate areas in which transparent, thermal-absorbent, and half-mirror glass are used. Transparent glass is used in the lower zone to avoid obstructing sight lines into the commercial facilities there. Two other kinds of glass are used in the upper regions as part of a thermal-energy policy. These materials help produce the image the building projects into the town setting.

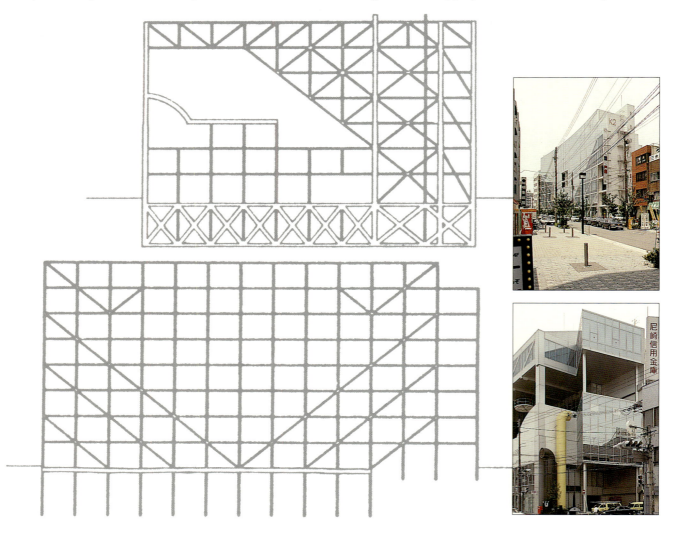

TAKEFUMI AIDA
SAITO MEMORIAL HALL, SHIBAURA INSTITUTE OF TECHNOLOGY, OMIYA

The site of Saito Memorial Hall is in the Omiya campus, where a suburban atmosphere still prevails. The campus was founded over 20 years ago and it was this plan which was adhered to in the construction of the Hall. Consequently, the relationship of the building to existing structures and the plaza it faces was carefully studied and the scenic composition of the campus was an important consideration .

Like trees observed in bright sunlight, the numerous wall planes give one the impression of wavering subtly, and the ones tipped three degrees reinforce this phenomenon. The walls, cut out at an angle of 45 degrees, endow space with movement and flow; they change in appearance depending on the movement of the observer; sometimes they seem like sharp lines, while at other times like solid masses. The wedge-shaped walls meanwhile are conceived as irregular elements introduced into these parallel systems.

The guest room is an alien presence; composed of reflective glass and aluminum panels, it is broken off at midpoint as it enters the classroom. The arrow-like form is intended to symbolise penetration – the mental acuity which this facility hopes to foster among students.

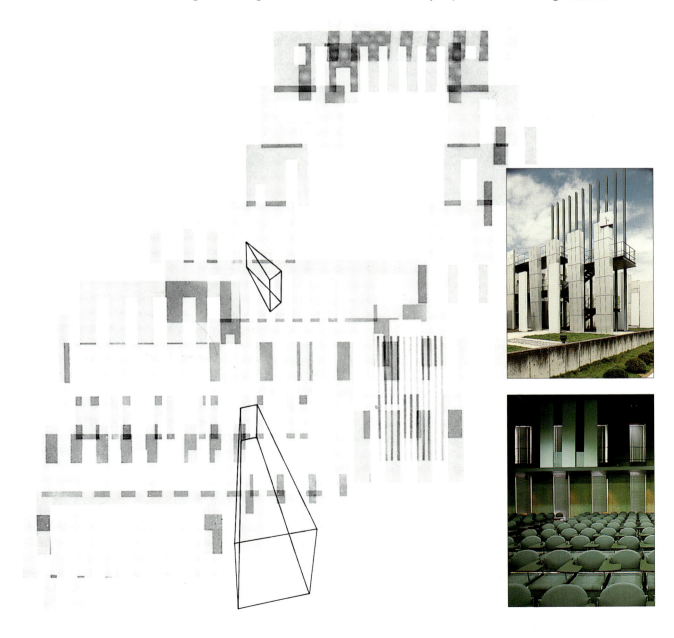

MINORU TAKEYAMA
TOKYO INTERNATIONAL PORT TERMINAL

Located in the southeast corner of Harumi, an early reclaimed 'island' within Tokyo bay and port, the Port Terminal Building (a competition winner) finds itself at the border of the city and the sea, man-made and natural landscapes, industrial and downtown areas; quite obviously, it is also a point of both departure and arrival. Accordingly, Takeyama has shaped the complex so that for those arriving from the sea, the structure could signify the point of landing or a 'landmark', while for those departing from here it could indicate the beginning of the sea and water, and so it is also a sea-mark or 'water-mark'. On the one hand the Terminal is articulated as a large house on top of a hill. Takeyama explains that the image of a house with a roof may appropriately signify arrival and home for those coming from the sea. On the other hand, for those coming from the land or the city, the building may appear as a structure on top of a cliff by the sea and so, like a lighthouse, it refers to the shore and the presence of the water. But the design does not lack the attributes of an oceanliner either: bridges, masts.

Indeed, Takeyama's architecture is imbued with dualities by both its location, function and its design. The building is comprised of two basic parts: a widespread solid base with extensive sloping edges plus a long balcony or terrace along the ship-in-port, and on top of this base structure a more geometrically shaped, cage-like struc-

ture which envelopes a glass box with four interconnected open domes. The four-storey lower base features large public spaces closely related to the Terminal's function: customs and immigration areas, meeting halls, lounges, etc, with parking spaces occupying the first floor underneath. On top of this base, Takeyama designed several large roof-top terraces which are directly accessible from the street through the numerous wide stairways that are prominent features of this part of the building. Circulation, nevertheless, is also a primary force in shaping the upper section. A pair of elevator-shafts, which thrust through the platform, are arranged alongside the 'house-like' tower, and are connected to it through two covered bridges on the fifth and sixth floors. The result, both in terms of form and structure, is somewhat reminiscent of certain Metabolist solutions (insofar as an independent system of circulation shafts was a trademark of Metabolism); however, it can equally remind one of certain Russian Constructivist projects as well.

Takeyama's scheme manages to combine the benefits of both urban and natural phenomena in a powerfully convincing way and turns the building into a lively place at the edge of the city. The Port Terminal is the first stage of a comprehensive redevelopment project of Harumi which will eventually convert the area into an attractive cultural, leisure and communication zone.

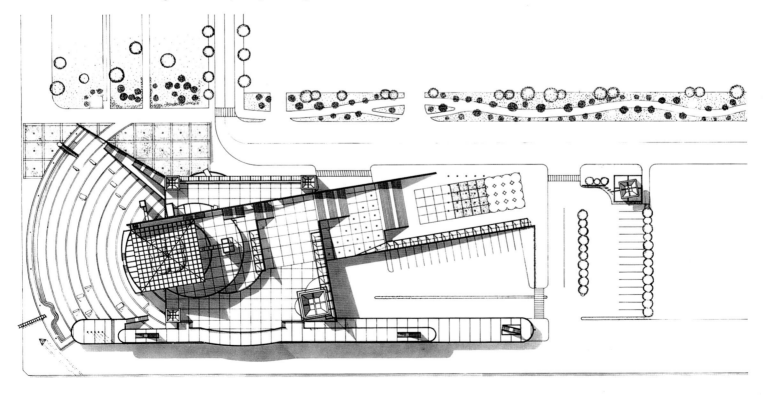

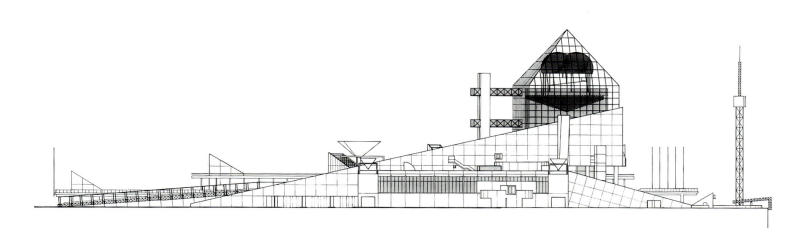

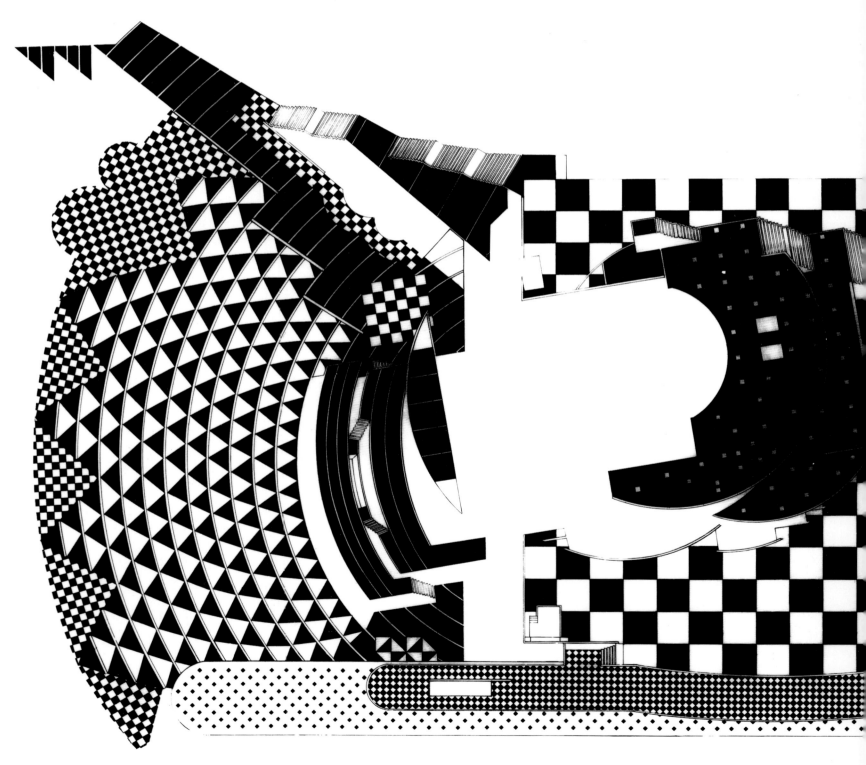

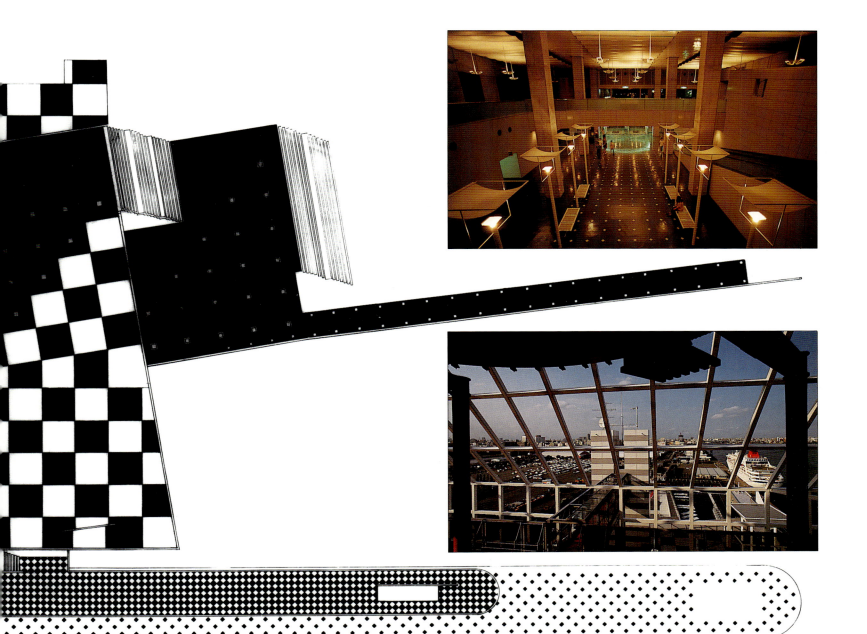

HIROSHI HARA
IIDA CITY MUSEUM

This building is a municipal cultural complex in Iida. It consists of an art museum, museum of regional natural history, multi-purpose gallery, auditorium and a planetarium. The art museum mainly exhibits the painting collection of Shunso Hishida, who was born in this city and is one of the Japanese artists represented.

Kunio Yanagida, the founder of Japanese folklore studies, was also born in Iida. His old house and that of another locally born poet were moved to, or reconstructed on this site. Together with several restored ruins of the Nagahime castle (moat, wells and water pipes), the whole site, that adjoins an old shrine, is designed as a museum park containing historical and local relics.

The roof terrace of this building, planned to become a part of this park, can be approached without entering the building. From here, one can view the Akaishi Mountains, commonly called the Southern Alps, which lie to the east. Iida is situated in the valley between this mountain range and another 3,000-metre range, the Central Alps. The sight of the Southern Alps is greatly cherished by the people here, and its silhouette inspired the design of the roof over the 80 metre-long main lobby. This roof, supported by tree-like concrete columns with steel trusses, was designed to evoke images of a forest, like those around the shrine, in the mountains, or in our memories.

The exhibition spaces required a controllable environment devoid of natural light, necessary for the preservation of delicate old Japanese paintings. The resulting uniformity and homogeneity of these spaces form the platform for the roof terrace and the main lobby which, conversely, are non-uniform, transient spaces, which change with the season, time and climate.

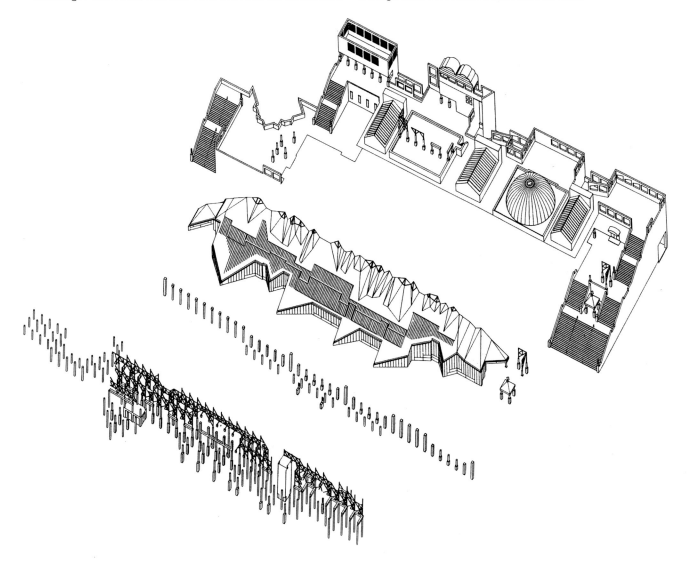

53

The site is in the centre of Himeji City, 500 metres to the northwest of Himeji Castle, at the foot of the hill known as Otokoyama. It is surrounded by a quiet residential district. From the verdant Otokoyama there is a view of Himeyama, the slope on which the castle sits. I wanted the architecture to reflect the topographical relationship between Otokoyama and Himeyama and to have this Museum of Literature harmonise with Himeji Castle, which is a superb landmark. The building is dedicated to the philosopher Tetsuro Watsuji. Its three floors and basement accommodate exhibition spaces, mainly for material on writers of this region, and a lecture hall. The building is in a garden with a man-made pond. In approaching the building, visitors have a distant view of the castle.

Two cubes, each 22.5 metres to a side and divided into nine parts, overlap at a 30 degree angle. One of the cubes is partly surrounded by a cylinder 20 metres in radius. There are ramps on both sides of the curving wall of the cylinder. Inside, there is an exhibition space, including a three-storey void. Visitors circulating inside and outside the building thus are provided with a dynamic spatial experience.

...ite is in the centre of Himeji City, 500 metres to the west of Himeji Castle, at the foot of the hill known as ...oyama. It is surrounded by a quiet residential district. ...the verdant Otokoyama there is a view of Himeyama, ...pe on which the castle sits. I wanted the architecture ...ect the topographical relationship between Otokoyama ...Himeyama and to have this Museum of Literature ...nise with Himeji Castle, which is a superb landmark. ... building is dedicated to the philosopher Tetsuro ...ji. Its three floors and basement accommodate ...ition spaces, mainly for material on writers of this region, and a lecture hall. The building is in a garden with a man-made pond. In approaching the building, visitors have a distant view of the castle.

Two cubes, each 22.5 metres to a side and divided into nine parts, overlap at a 30 degree angle. One of the cubes is partly surrounded by a cylinder 20 metres in radius. There are ramps on both sides of the curving wall of the cylinder. Inside, there is an exhibition space, including a three-storey void. Visitors circulating inside and outside the building thus are provided with a dynamic spatial experience.

TADAO ANDO
MUSEUM OF LITERATURE, HIMEJI

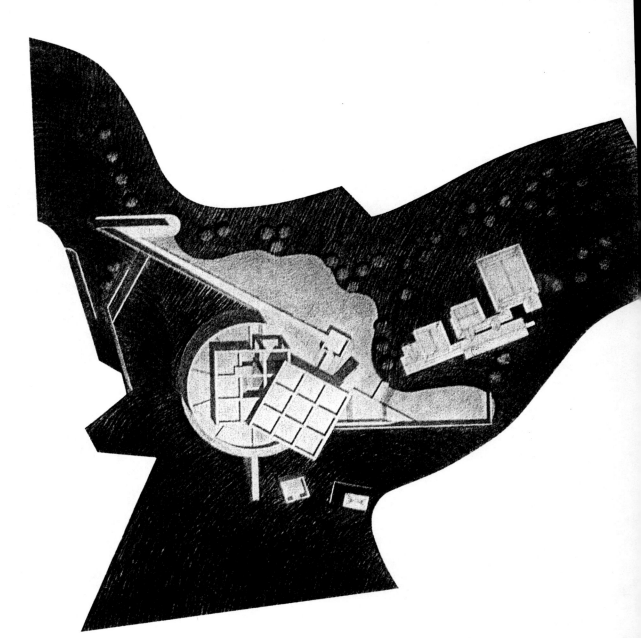

...ite is in the centre of Himeji City, 500 metres to the west of Himeji Castle, at the foot of the hill known as ...oyama. It is surrounded by a quiet residential district. ...the verdant Otokoyama there is a view of Himeyama, ...pe on which the castle sits. I wanted the architecture ...ct the topographical relationship between Otokoyama ...imeyama and to have this Museum of Literature ...nise with Himeji Castle, which is a superb landmark. ...e building is dedicated to the philosopher Tetsuro ...ji. Its three floors and basement accommodate ...ition spaces, mainly for material on writers of this region, and a lecture hall. The building is in a garden with a man-made pond. In approaching the building, visitors have a distant view of the castle.

Two cubes, each 22.5 metres to a side and divided into nine parts, overlap at a 30 degree angle. One of the cubes is partly surrounded by a cylinder 20 metres in radius. There are ramps on both sides of the curving wall of the cylinder. Inside, there is an exhibition space, including a three-storey void. Visitors circulating inside and outside the building thus are provided with a dynamic spatial experience.

The site is in the centre of Himeji City, 500 metres to the northwest of Himeji Castle, at the foot of the hill known as Otokoyama. It is surrounded by a quiet residential district. From the verdant Otokoyama there is a view of Himeyama, the slope on which the castle sits. I wanted the architecture to reflect the topographical relationship between Otokoyama and Himeyama and to have this Museum of Literature harmonise with Himeji Castle, which is a superb landmark.

The building is dedicated to the philosopher Tetsuro Watsuji. Its three floors and basement accommodate exhibition spaces, mainly for material on writers of this region, and a lecture hall. The building is in a garden with a man-made pond. In approaching the building, visitors have a distant view of the castle.

Two cubes, each 22.5 metres to a side and divided into nine parts, overlap at a 30 degree angle. One of the cubes is partly surrounded by a cylinder 20 metres in radius. There are ramps on both sides of the curving wall of the cylinder. Inside, there is an exhibition space, including a three-storey void. Visitors circulating inside and outside the building thus are provided with a dynamic spatial experience.

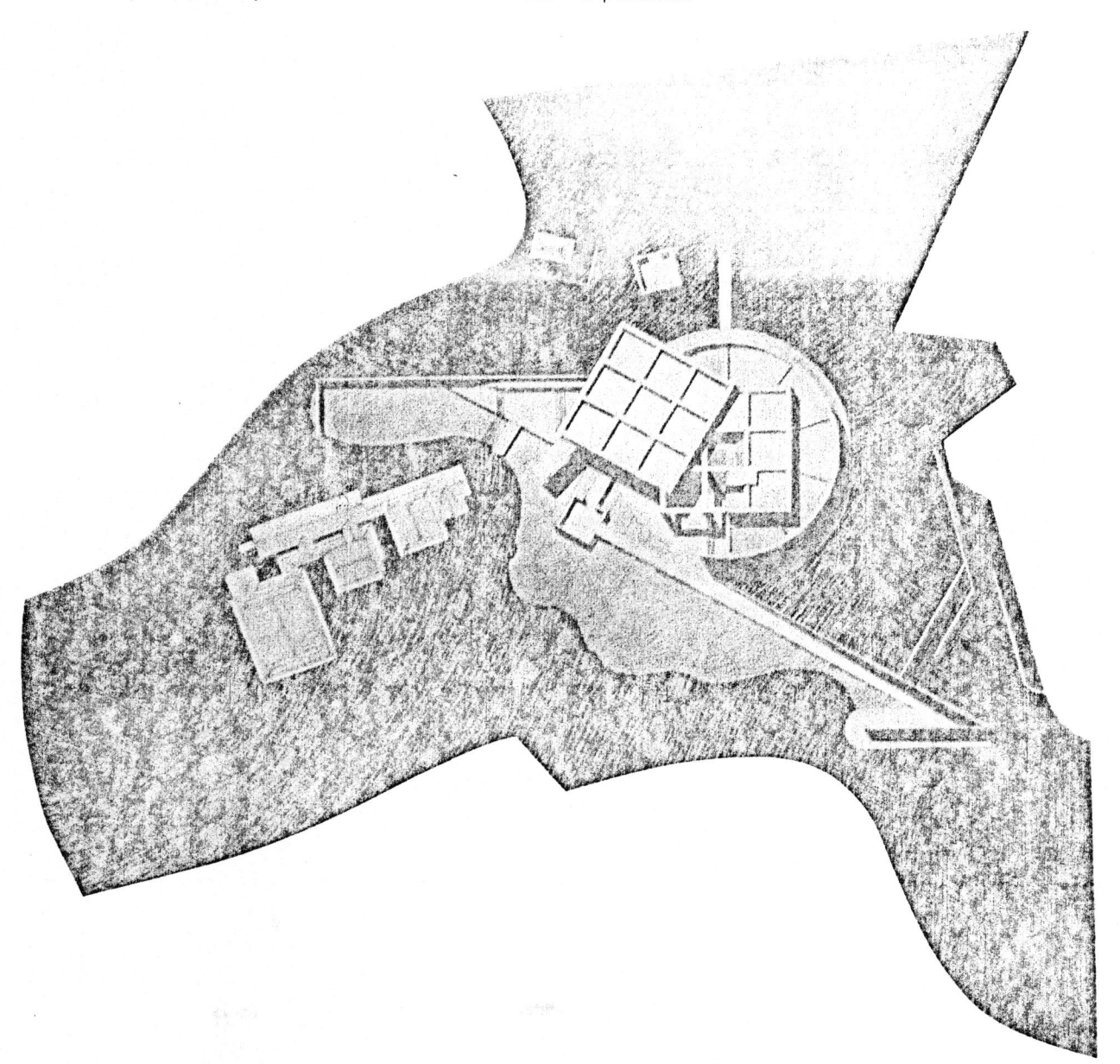

te is in the centre of Himeji City, 500 metres to the est of Himeji Castle, at the foot of the hill known as yama. It is surrounded by a quiet residential district. he verdant Otokoyama there is a view of Himeyama, pe on which the castle sits. I wanted the architecture ct the topographical relationship between Otokoyama imeyama and to have this Museum of Literature nise with Himeji Castle, which is a superb landmark. building is dedicated to the philosopher Tetsuro i. Its three floors and basement accommodate ion spaces, mainly for material on writers of this region, and a lecture hall. The building is in a garden with a man-made pond. In approaching the building, visitors have a distant view of the castle.

Two cubes, each 22.5 metres to a side and divided into nine parts, overlap at a 30 degree angle. One of the cubes is partly surrounded by a cylinder 20 metres in radius. There are ramps on both sides of the curving wall of the cylinder. Inside, there is an exhibition space, including a three-storey void. Visitors circulating inside and outside the building thus are provided with a dynamic spatial experience.

TADAO ANDO
MUSEUM OF LITERATURE, HIMEJI

The site is in the centre of Himeji City, 500 metres to the northwest of Himeji Castle, at the foot of the hill known as Otokoyama. It is surrounded by a quiet residential district. From the verdant Otokoyama there is a view of Himeyama, the slope on which the castle sits. I wanted the architecture to reflect the topographical relationship between Otokoyama and Himeyama and to have this Museum of Literature harmonise with Himeji Castle, which is a superb landmark.

The building is dedicated to the philosopher Tetsuro Watsuji. Its three floors and basement accommodate exhibition spaces, mainly for material on writers of this region, and a lecture hall. The building is in a garden with a man-made pond. In approaching the building, visitors have a distant view of the castle.

Two cubes, each 22.5 metres to a side and divided into nine parts, overlap at a 30 degree angle. One of the cubes is partly surrounded by a cylinder 20 metres in radius. There are ramps on both sides of the curving wall of the cylinder. Inside, there is an exhibition space, including a three-storey void. Visitors circulating inside and outside the building thus are provided with a dynamic spatial experience.

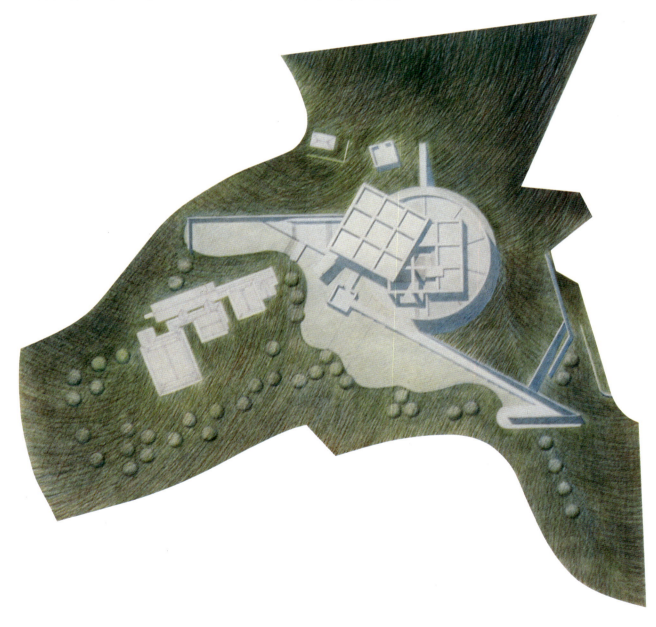

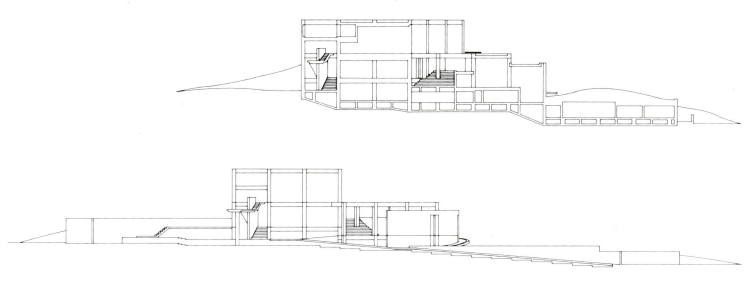

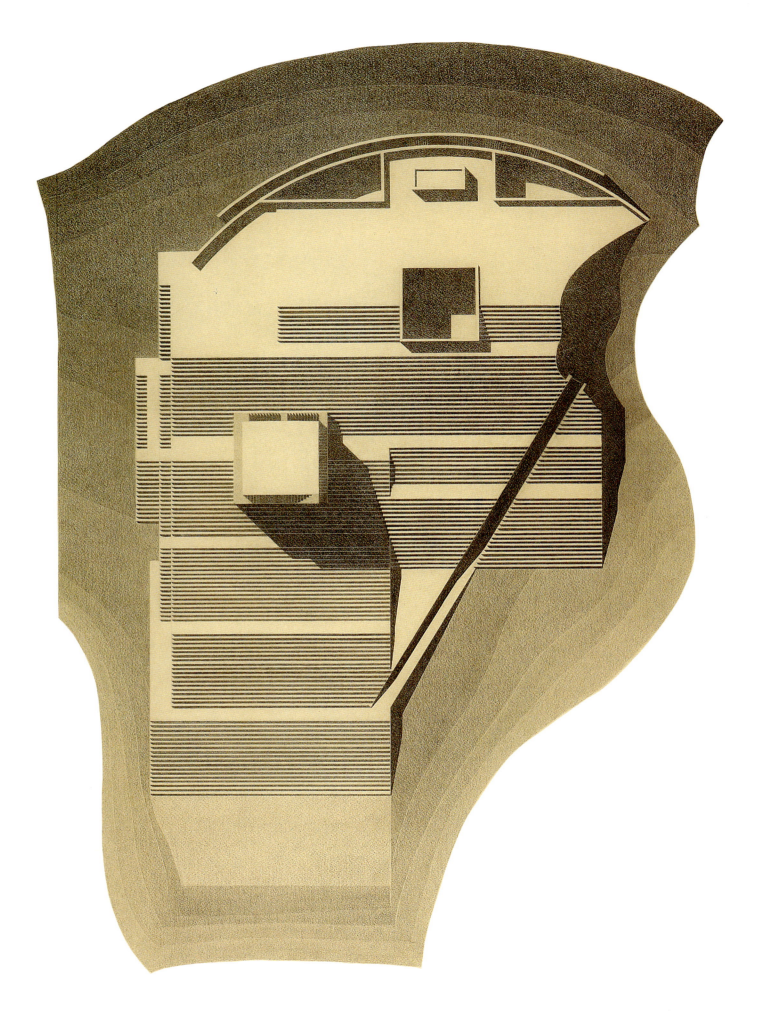

56

CHIKATSU-ASUKA HISTORIC MUSEUM, OSAKA

Chikatsu-Asuka, an area in the southern part of Osaka Prefecture, has one of the best collections of tumuli (*kofun*) in Japan. There are over 200 mounds including four imperial tombs, the site of the tomb of Prince Shotoku and the tomb of Ono-no-Imoko. The area was an important place at the beginning of Japanese history.

Our project is a museum for exhibiting and studying the *kofun* culture. In contrast to past museums, this will not be just a facility for exhibiting unearthed objects. As a part of a new endeavour, it will also introduce and show the entire group of tumuli scattered over the area. For this reason, the building has been conceived as a hill from which one can see the entire excavated area.

The stepped up structure is to provide a view of the surrounding tumuli that stretch across a basin. Nearby are a grove of plum trees and a pond, and around it are paths over the hills mentioned in the *Fudoki*. This museum is to be enveloped by a rich natural environment. In early spring the attraction is the blossoming plum trees, in early summer there is the new greenery, and in autumn the foliage paints the area in vivid colours. The building will become a centre of outdoor activities and will no doubt function as the nucleus of the region. The stepped roof will also be used as a plaza for viewing drama and music festivals, various performances, and lectures.

Inside the building, darkness spreads. The unearthed objects are exhibited in the same way as they were found in the tumuli. People therefore experience the sensation of entering a *kofun*. A visit to the building represents a journey to the underworld of ancient times. This is a place where the Japanese could encounter their own history; it is a 'tumulus' built in the present Heisei era (1989), dedicated to the Japanese love of nature.

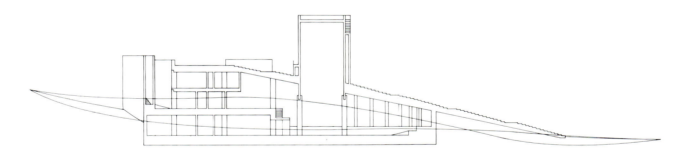

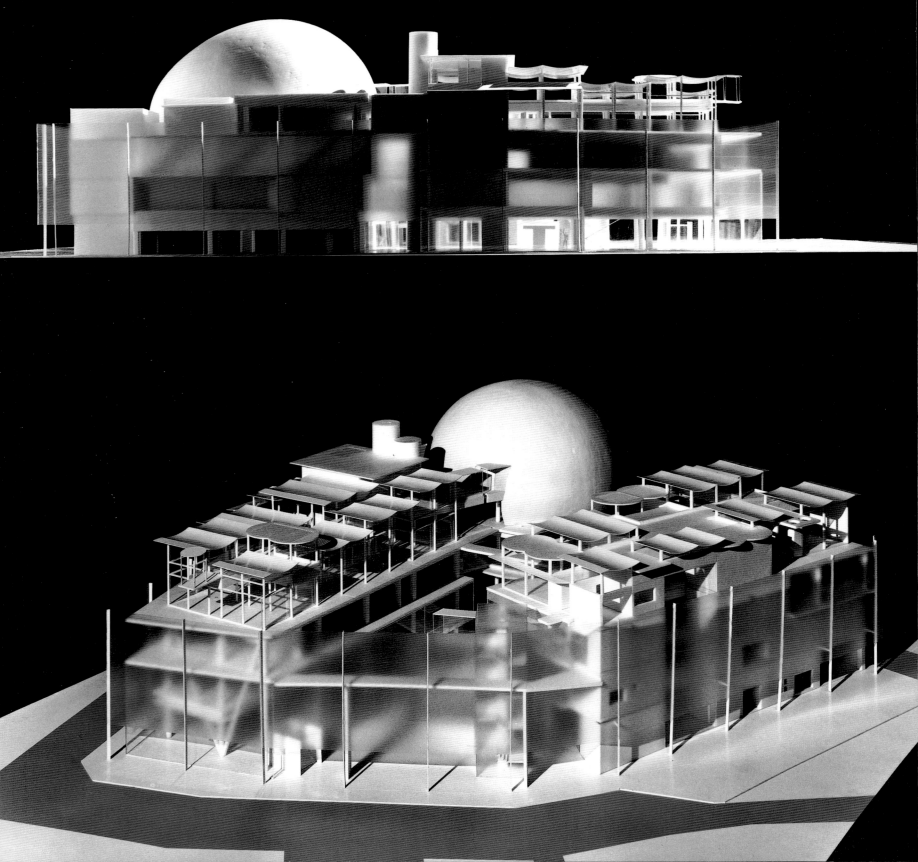

ITSUKO HASEGAWA
'SUMIDA' METAPHORICAL TOWNSCAPE, TOKYO

Sumida Ward is an area of traditional working-class neighbourhoods in Tokyo, where the old popular culture lives on and many kinds of traditional handicrafts are still practised. Much of the history of Tokyo is preserved there, and consequently the area has a distinctive quality. I felt that the Culture and Learning Centre must be rooted in this area. As in many neighbourhoods, small houses are clustered close together around the site.

The centre had to be in harmony with the area and not create a totally alien townscape. On a site that was not quite quadrangular, I arranged three separate volumes to form a plaza. This plaza connects with two neighbourhood streets, facilitating movement in the area. The southwest volume accommodates assembly and communication spaces, a hall and a planetarium. The southeast volume contains an information centre and a library above the entrance hall. The third volume has study rooms and a branch office of the ward council, and on the top floor are counselling rooms for children who have problems adapting to their social environment. The parts are linked by bridges that help expand the services provided by the centre. Each volume is defined by translucent screens which lend an order but do not close off spaces entirely in what is a crowded area. The layered translucent screens articulate space in ways that suggest traditional features such as *shoji*, *sudare* and *koshido*.

Another theme is the expression of people's movement. This centre has many complex activities and spaces, which must be both separated and related. The many bridges above the plaza and the elevator and steps facing the plaza express movement and the relationships among activities. Most places in the building have views of the plaza. The movement of the public and events and performances in the plaza are all visible. Stalls dubbed 'Sumida showcases', in which craftsmen can work or where displays of traditional handicrafts can be arranged, are provided. There is also a stream flowing through the area. A typical scene in the back streets of old Sumida, with the Sumida River and nature close by, is suggested.

During the planning and design of this building, the traditional Japanese community provided a metaphor, and aspects of it were translated into modern or futuristic forms. These forms are abstract and simple, yet they fit into the neighbourhood. At the same time, they stimulate and invigorate the area.

Tokyo is flooded with information. This centre helps to keep up with that information while transmitting new messages of its own.

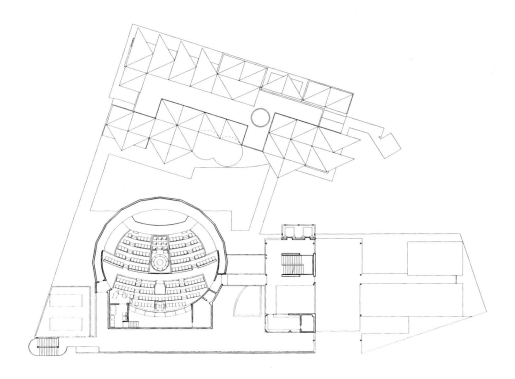

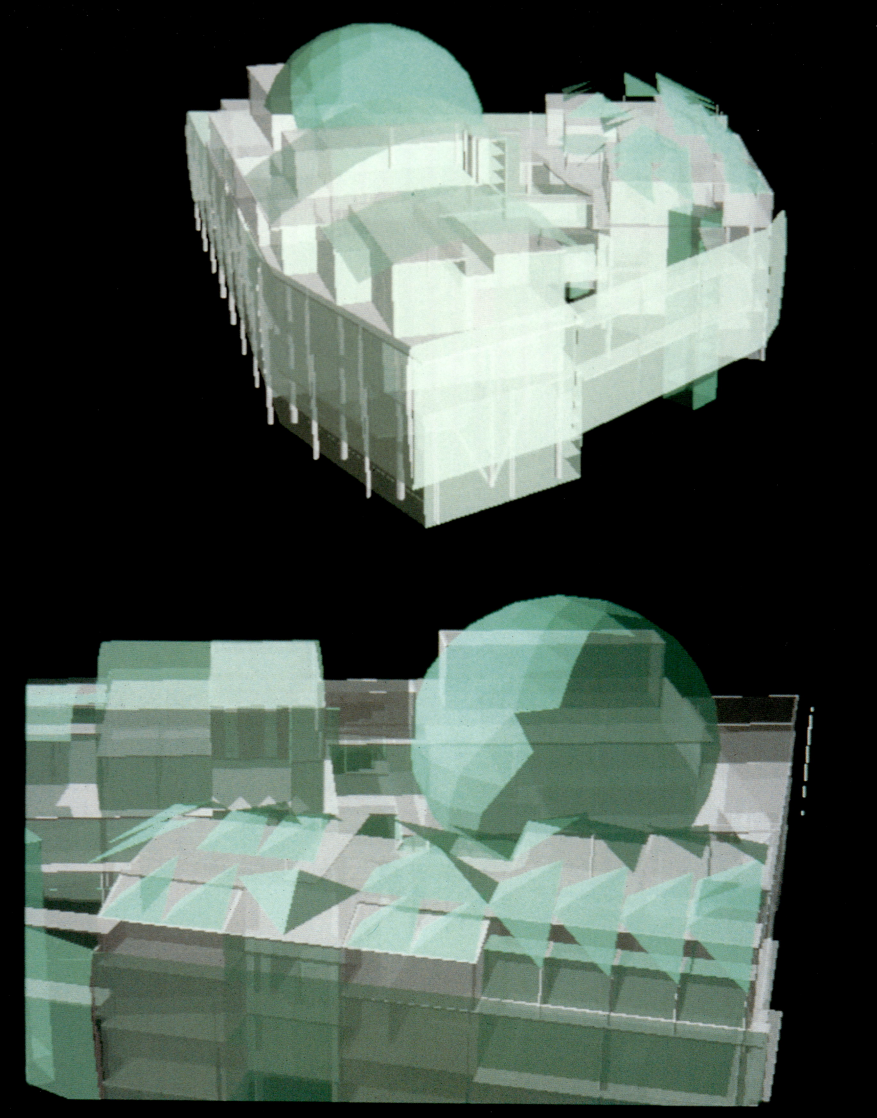

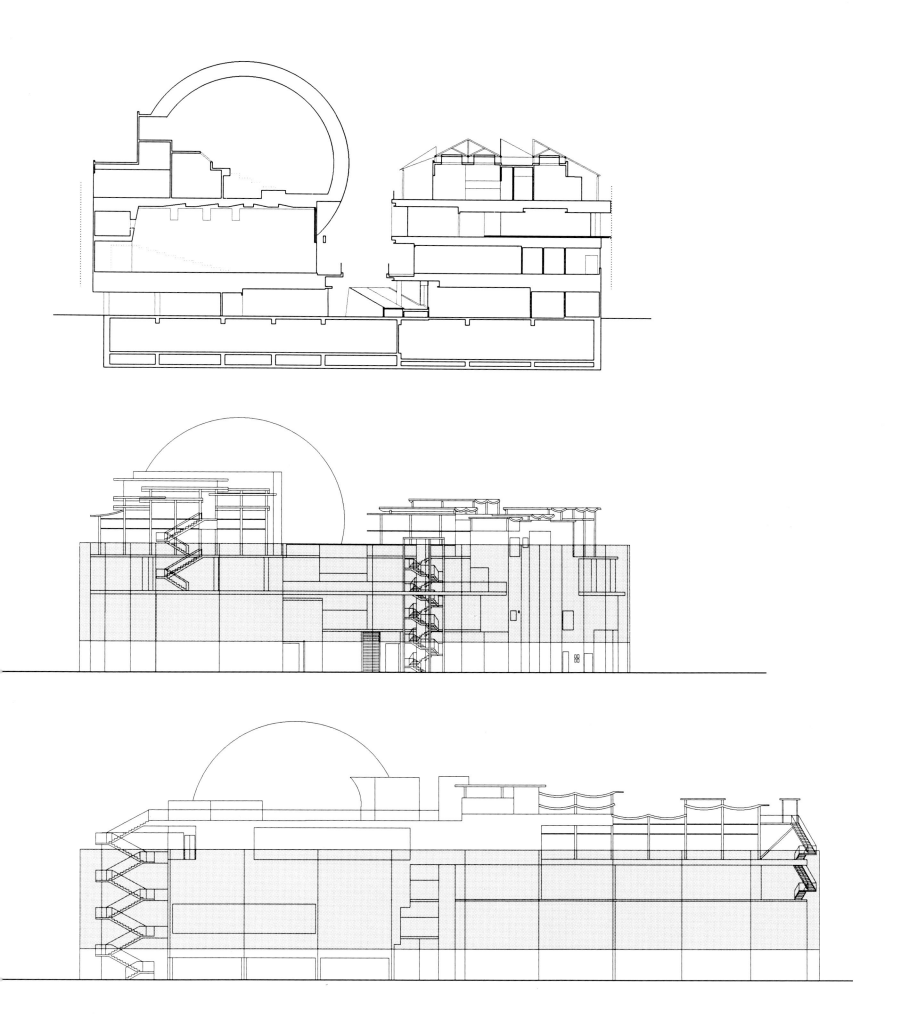

TOYO ITO
SAPPORO BEER GUEST HOUSE, ENIWA, HOKKAIDO

Beer breweries and food factories are scattered on the bleak and flat land along Highway 36, which extends from Chitose Airport to Sapporo City. Sapporo Breweries' plant is one of them and has a vast area of approximately 300,000 squares metres.

Its guest house, planned to accommodate visitors to the plant, is built in the garden which occupies a third of the area, or about 100,000 square metres. We were asked to participate in the joint project with Y Uemura of Sapporo Breweries, Y Ueda of Ueda Culture Projects, S Fukukawa, a landscape designer, and Y Kanno, a composer.

The route from the entrance of the plant to the garden was designed to flow and the guest house was planned as an element en route. The large scale garden is comprised of the Pond of Odin, the Hill of Elm Trees, the Wood of Fairies, the Plaza of Fire, and the Marshland, in the image of Scandinavian landscape.

The guest house was designed to face a shell-like sunken garden and almost everything, except for moderately curved walls and approach, is buried underground to blend with the surrounding topography. The house appears more like a piece of earthwork than as architecture.

The plan is finished as a set of polygonal spaces with apexes associated by geometric rule rather than form. Various functions including a bar, restaurant, and sitting area are assigned to respective unit spaces and finished with skylights, ceiling frescoes, and textile coverings, which are effective in their varied expressions.

A ventilating tower, skylights, and entrance canopy which appear above the ground have a common design, suggesting wings of an aeroplane, to form a landscape. The extensive walls encircling the plaza are provided with punched metal facade screens to soften their otherwise monotonous expression.

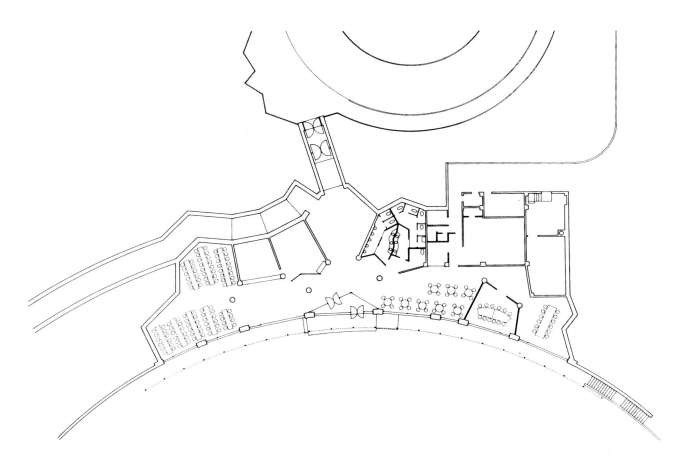

ABOVE: REFLECTED CEILING PLAN

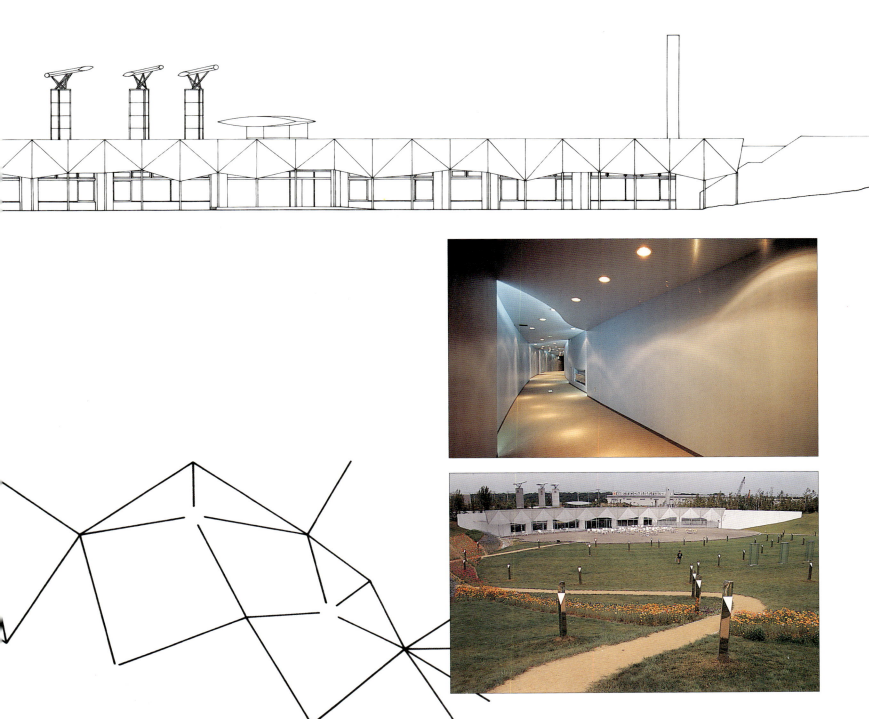

Yatsushiro is 40 kilometres south of Kumamoto City, which stands amidst the rich nature of mountains, river and sea. The site is near the former castle, where many of the city's cultural facilities are situated. Across the street is the Edo Shohin-ken villa, the flat, horizontal line of which seemed to be a significant idiom to apply to the project.

We were concerned about the large volume of the building which had to be built three storeys high. Our efforts were, therefore, concentrated on solving various complicated functional problems and creating human-scale spaces suitable for people to meet in. Our solution was to place both the main exhibition room, with the largest enclosure, and the administration/service office on the first floor; the entrance, café, and citizen's gallery, which are more or less open spaces, on the second floor; and

storage on the third floor. The first floor is underground, buried by artificially raised and landscaped earthwork covering a large area in front. Consequently, there is an excellent view from the second floor over this man-made hill that slopes to the ground level.

The structure fuses, and/or contrasts the with the landscape in an attempt to create a new environmental architecture. The softly-shaped section of the archives and storage on the top floor evokes the image of a warehouse, which is a customary adjunct to a museum, rather than to an exhibition. It is expected that upon viewing this 'floating', shiny, metallic volume, one will be prompted to find an association between nature and artifice. The man-made hill, which acts as a bridge, performs a similar function.

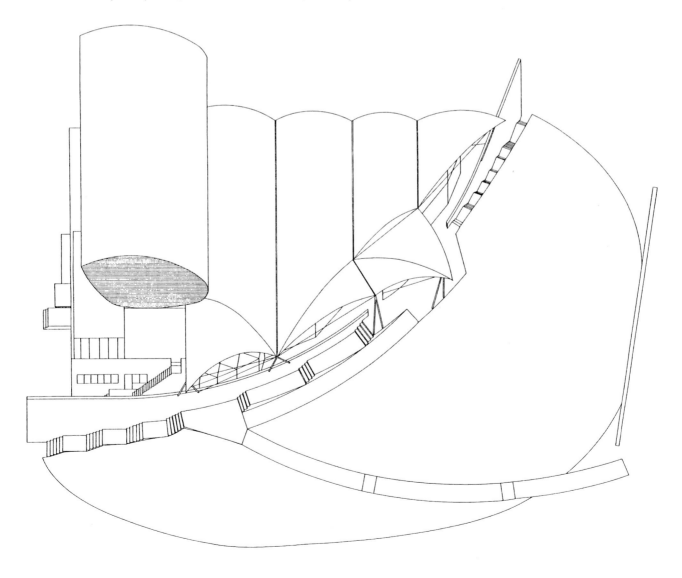

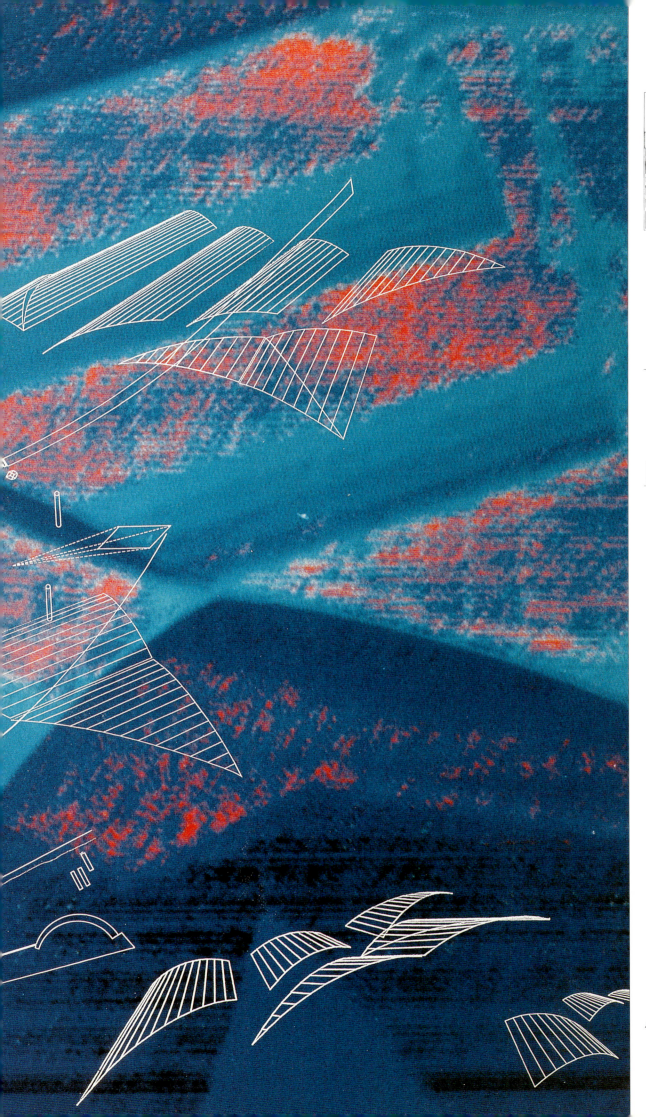

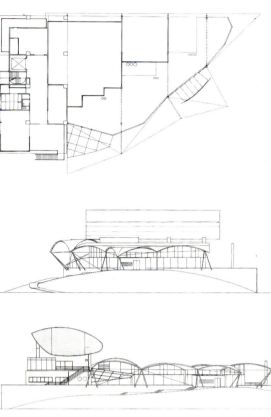

ABOVE: third-floor plan and elevations

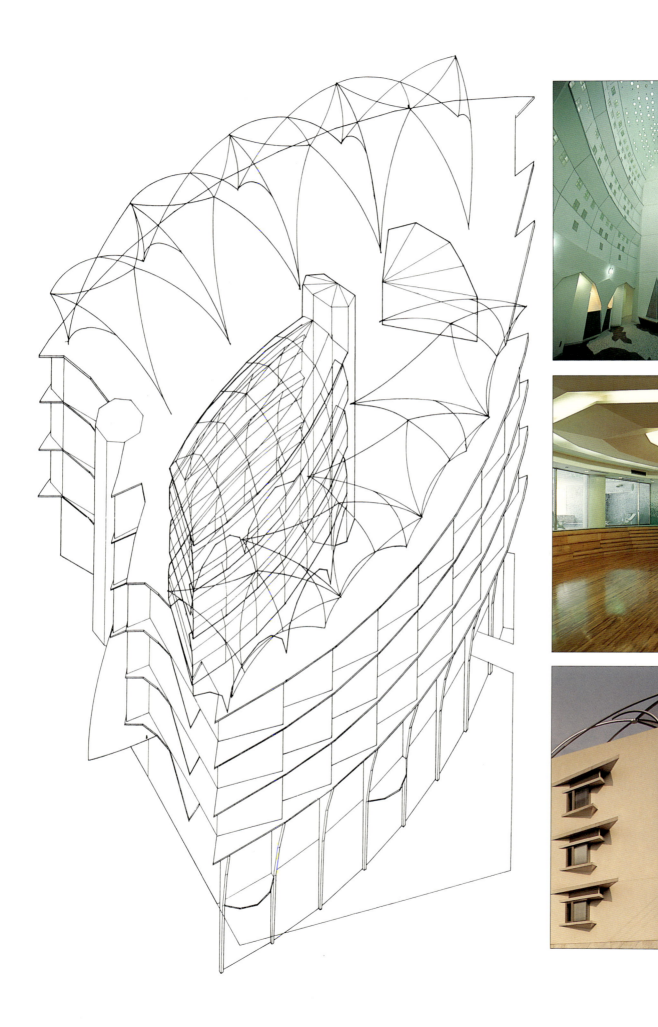

YASUMITSU MATSUNAGA
Y'S COURT NAKAHARA, KAWASAKI

This project started when the client, a developer, commissioned us to propose an ideal dormitory for their staff. The design is meant to serve as a model for this building type which is highly demanded in Japan as a viable means of attracting the ever-decreasing young labour force. We regarded this project as a continuation of our previous studies in the field of collective housing which, generally speaking, has had strong negative connotations in Japan in comparison with individual dwellings because of the over-exaggeration of the merits of privacy and exclusive ownership of land. However, the recent soar of land prices has forced more and more people to live collectively, and we have been involved in a number of housing projects in search of more positive aspects of living together.

The site is located in a mixed-use area in Kawasaki nicknamed 'Japanese silicon valley'. The only requirement given by the client was the capacity of some 50 unmarried employees. Within the tight envelope stipulated by strict zoning regulations, efforts to provide rooms with maximum exposure to the exterior resulted in an oval outline containing a lofty atrium in the centre. This atrium acts as a mental symbol of the integration of the residents living on several floors.

The private rooms are equipped with a shower-room, walk-in closet, and balcony. In addition, there is a community dining room, lounge, sauna, jetbath, swimming pool, gymnasium, play room, automated parking system, and other such facilities which modern young Japanese would dream of having. Residents enjoy their life here as if staying in a resort hotel. This sort of leisurely lifestyle is only possible for young people by living in a dormitory as a form of collective housing in our country of sky-high land prices.

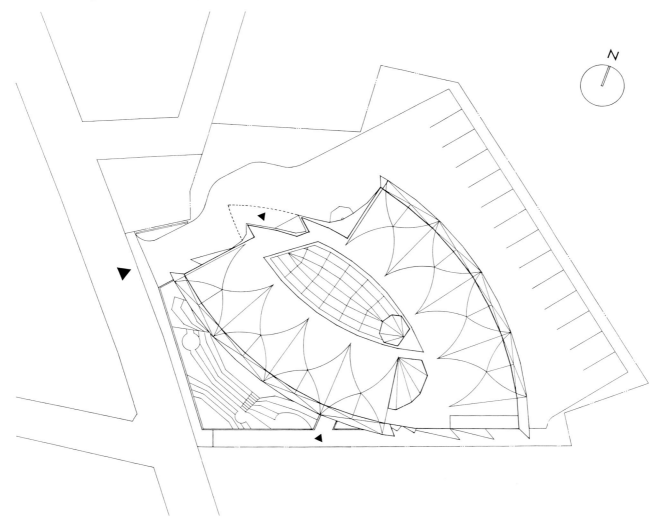

RYOJI SUZUKI
KOUNJI TEMPLE, TOKYO

The essence of the overall plan of the Temple is based upon our 'Void of Missing Link Model No 6' (for the five previous works so far attempted in Tokyo we employed five different types of such model), developed to position architecture into the Japanese city structure.

One of the distinct features of Japanese cities is a system of extremely tight gaps or empty spaces between buildings that define the boundaries of private properties usually existing without any function or effective use of space. Cities in Japan are therefore covered by a network of these innumerable voids and our own 'void'consciously attempts to handle this network.

The 'void of the missing link' consists of orbits with various curvatures and 'axes'. In planning, we select the 'VML model' most suitable to the site and try to place space over the line or over the segments of the arc and internalise them. This allows architecture to embrace the void of the Japanese city internally while, at the same time, it releases architecture towards this chaotic network of void in the city.

Designing a temple today entails some degree of political conflict between 'modern' and 'traditional' principles. However, what we have attempted here was to subtract the 'principle' from both and let them function on the same stage at the same time. What we found to be required here was 'observation' rather than 'creation'.

SHIN TAKAMATSU
SOLARIS BUILDING, AMAGASAKI, HYOGO

It will be difficult to guess the use of this building from its exterior. In fact, apart from the common parking in the basement, there will be a great variety of facilities, with a supermarket at street level, a café above that, and even a Chinese restaurant on the third floor. Located in the outskirts of Osaka, the site occupies a favourable position in front of a station of a private railway company, in a new town where there has been a rapid increase in the population over the last few years, most of the people being from the younger generation. The usual way to plan a commercial building is first to survey potential customer types and then, having established the market to be strategically targeted, detailed decisions are made about the composition of what is to be offered as well as about the interior design and the design of the building itself, while taking into account the preferences and popular trends affecting the targeted customer group as part of the whole process of investigation. However, the methodology adopted in the case of this project was different. Apart from several areas in which there was a general understanding, schemes for each of the undertakings concerned were developed independently and, at a certain point in their development, forcibly bundled up with the idea of intentionally knitting them together, while trying to make the best use of the conflicts inevitably generated between each of them.

The kind of adjustments which are essential with a more normal planning technique are actually a kind of 'cover up job' to conceal those points where there is no continuity, or more simply speaking, it is a process of necessary compromise. But with the process of working which we had elected to use, we soon realised that the points of fission between each of the schemes was the hidden key to a completely new and highly attractive line of development. In this connection, the interiors of the second and third floors are being designed by the French designer, Jean-Michel Wilmotte, who has produced a highly individual space almost completely unrelated to the particular features of the building. Therefore, if the way in which customers are attracted to each of the schemes is different, there will also be an infinite variety in the way each of the designers has considered those spaces, remembering that the schemes may even be conflicting with the keynote of the project as a whole. It also goes without saying, of course, that people, anyway, have different tastes in design. Thus, main themes, narratives and even rhetoric will differ, and the resulting diverse contextual framework created will be akin to a frantic, and yet synchronised ballet of literary space. With such a situation as this, there is always the hope that some kind of unexpected story of literary proportions will develop, full of uncertainty and expectation. Even if there is only one person who is unaware of what is happening, it will be enough. With this particular building, therefore, we were much more interested in the thinking behind Modern art and the ideas of Franz Kafka, than in architectural design, means and techniques *per se*.

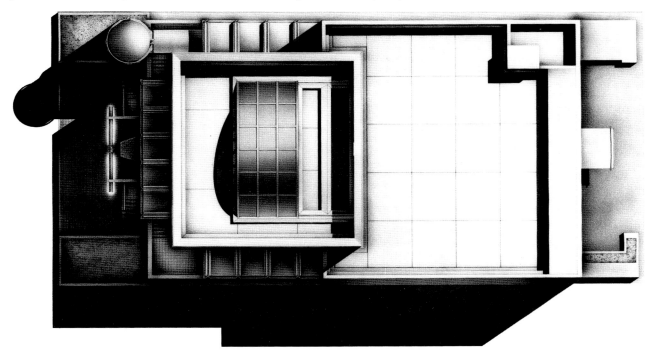

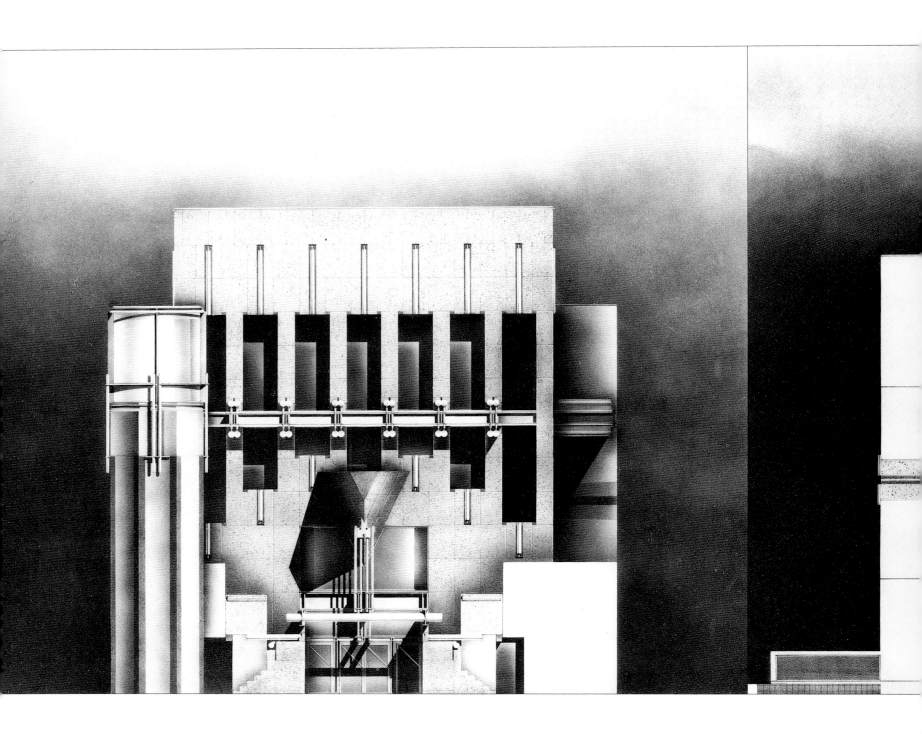

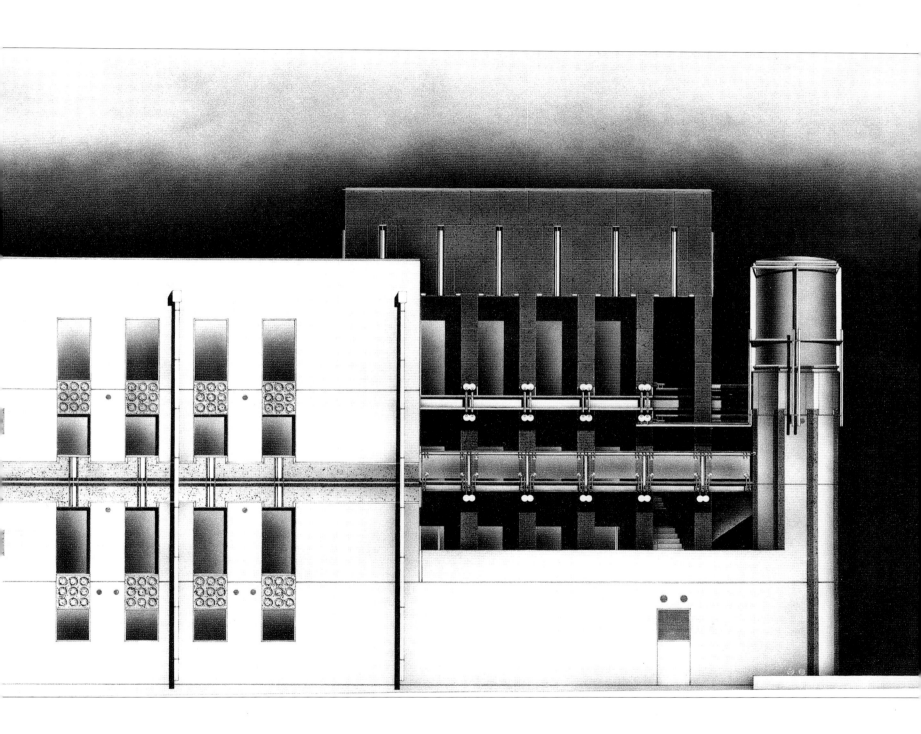

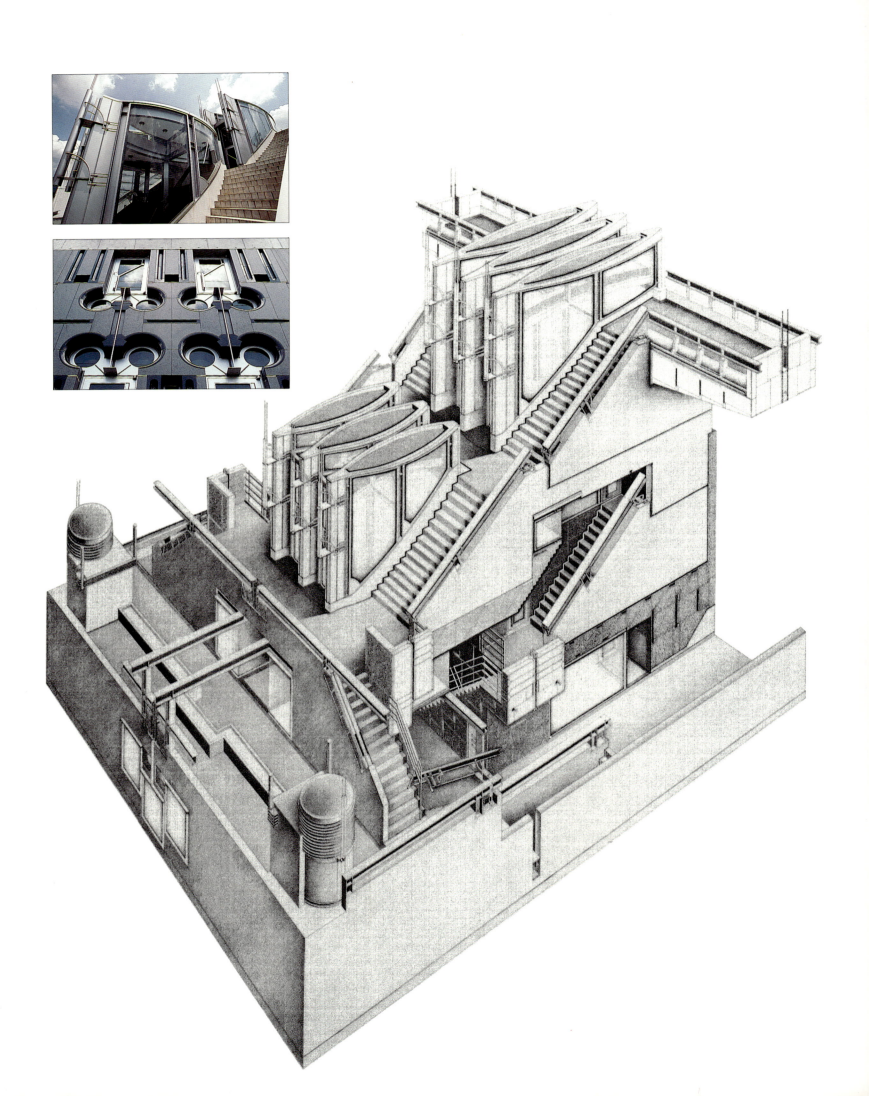

SYNTAX BUILDING, KYOTO

Kitayama-dori is a street about 800-metres long in the northern extremity of the city of Kyoto. During the past four or five years many new buildings have been built on the north side of the street, where they overlook the expanse of a botanical garden on the south. Though very pleasant and green, the neighbourhood lacks the bustle of city streets. Syntax is the fourth of the buildings we have designed for this compact district – at a rate of about one a year.

The flashy Week (1986), which we built at the west end of the road about five years ago, initiated a change in the appearance of Kitayama-dori. In 1990, we finished Oxy, located about 300 metres east of Week at roughly the middle point of Kitayama-dori. Because of its functions, this building is more moderate in appearance than its more boldly designed neighbours on both sides. East of Oxy, after a small dull stretch of scenery, just at the eastern end of the botanical garden, stands Inning 23, completed three years ago, in 1988. Although when it was finished its height and imposing appearance made it conspicuous, it

no longer seems the case. It is now in the category of average Kitayama-dori design.

Located diagonally across the street from it, Syntax, another building of fashion retail stores, was begun just as Inning 23 was approaching completion. Although we did not foresee such a thing, we have ended up planning four buildings within a distance of a few hundred metres. Because of its location at the east end of the street, we wanted to give Syntax a conspicuous design that would suggest a kind of termination and would tell the tale of this compact street in a terse fashion.

It takes only about ten minutes to walk from one end to the other, but the street has great magnetic charm. We were not asked to relate these four buildings in any specific way to a single context. The owners are all different, and it was almost coincidental that we were entrusted with all of them. For this reason, each is complete within its own system and plays an important part in the freedom and flexibility of the story of Kitayama-dori.

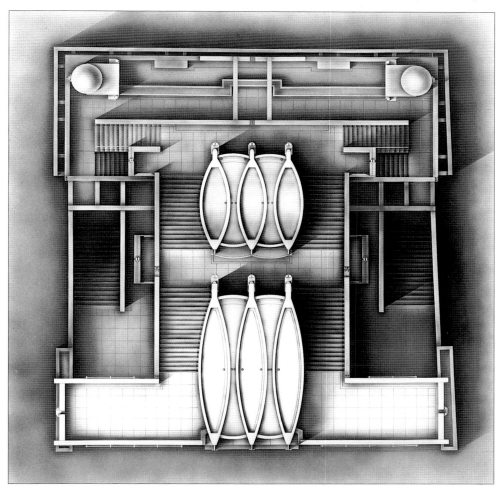

ATSUSHI KITAGAWARA
METROTOUR (EDOKEN) BUILDING, TOKYO

A corporate headquarters building in downtown Tokyo, the 11-storey structure is covered with a Belgian glass curtain-wall that imparts slight curves to the overall facade. Projecting catwalks for glass maintenance suggest the wings of a dragonfly. A breeze of 'electronic wind' flows through the entrance hall lobby, and lights (cast aluminium drapes) rustle in the wind. These features overcome the solidity of the built form.

Ideas arising in the design process generally seem to have coalesced around a critical representation of Tokyo as an 'evanescent' or ephemeral city. The phenomenological awareness informing design here is that Tokyo is a series of events, like air, wind, or insubstantiality. Constantin Brancusi's *Bird in Space* is the motif for this architecture. No mere analogy, here such aspiration to flight and lightness have a keen and profound meaning that gives perceptible form, or imagery to the invisible forces regulating the constitution of Tokyo's urban space.

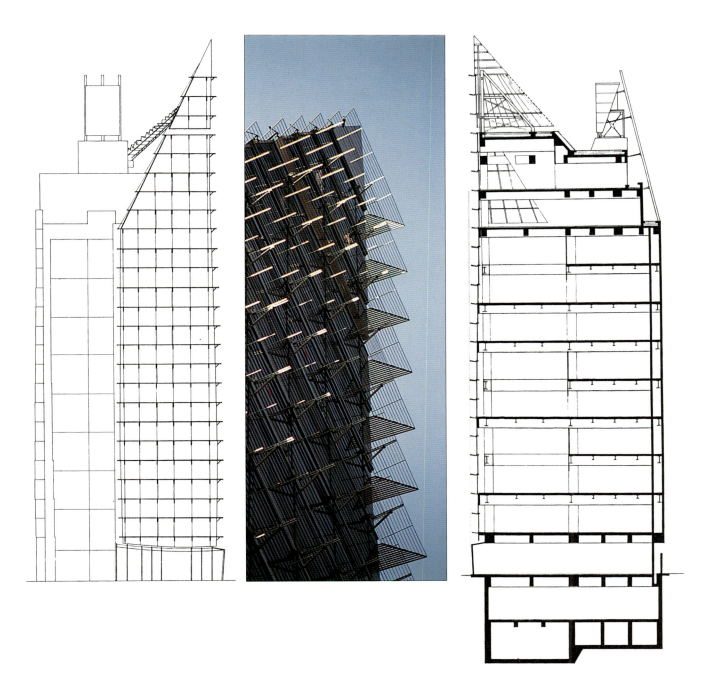

SANTO BUILDING, KYOTO

There is an infinite number of tiny gardens in the city of Kyoto. These 'micro-gardens' provide much needed modulations of the city's spatial structure. Surrounded by reinforced glass screens with supports of glittering mushroom-shaped aluminium casting, in the micro-garden of Santo – a small home appliance showroom and office building – a myriad of things are arranged to bustle in sublime excess. Yet every single event: the steep, grassy slope, the slim, black granite bridge with its suspended, stainless steel canopy, the flights of stairs partially covered by blue, metallic surfaces, the airy, steel terrace suspended in mid-air, etc, has its own place. This tiny garden could be seen as Lautréamont's *tokonoma* bathed in crisp morning sunlight.

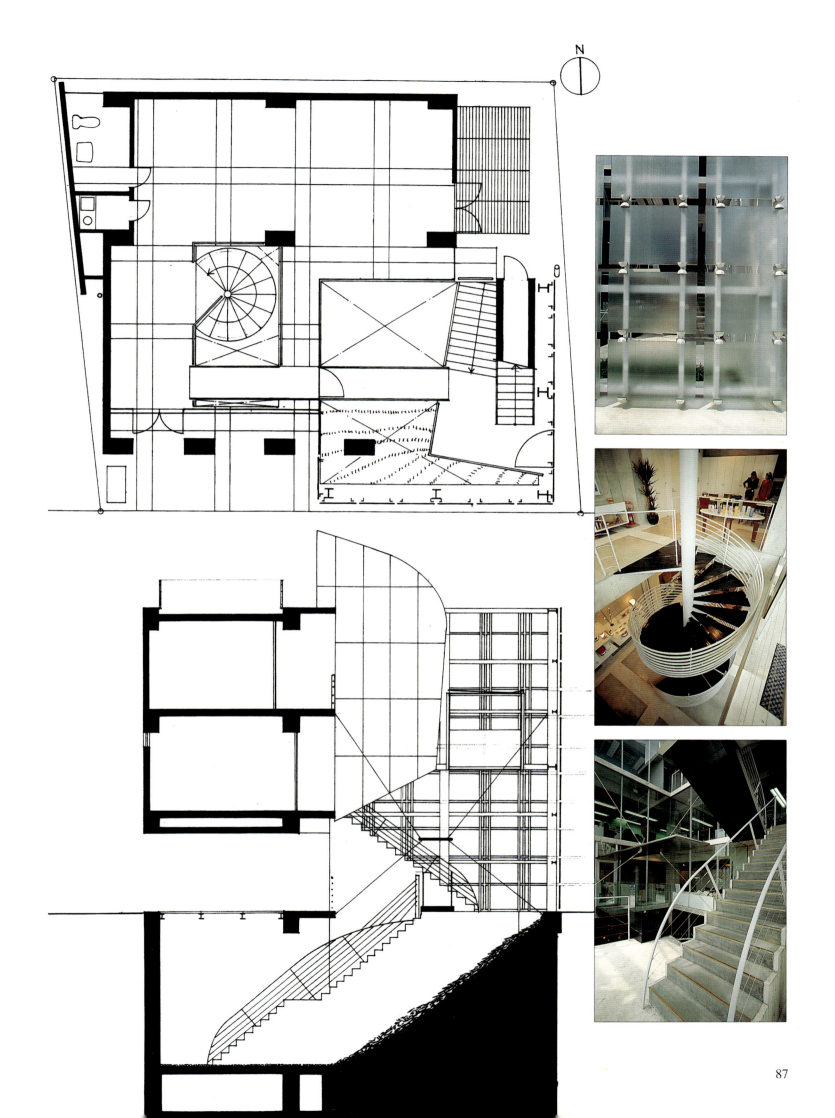

HAJIME YATSUKA
WING BUILDING, NISHINOMIYA, HYOGO

The Wing is a small retail complex of fashion stores and boutiques located along a major road near the station of Shukugawa in Nishinomiya city. Using the unique characteristics of the corner site, I have designed the building with a wedge-shaped wing in the front. Another, negative wedge is driven between the interior and outside stairs with a bridge connection. Hovering above these wedges, I devised a double canopy, something like wings. The big, partially enclosed void carved into the building attracts people who pass by, while producing a theatrical space *à la* Piranesi. The volumes on either side of this open atrium, along with the use of various kinds of materials, figures and signage ensure further the effectiveness of this new urban space.

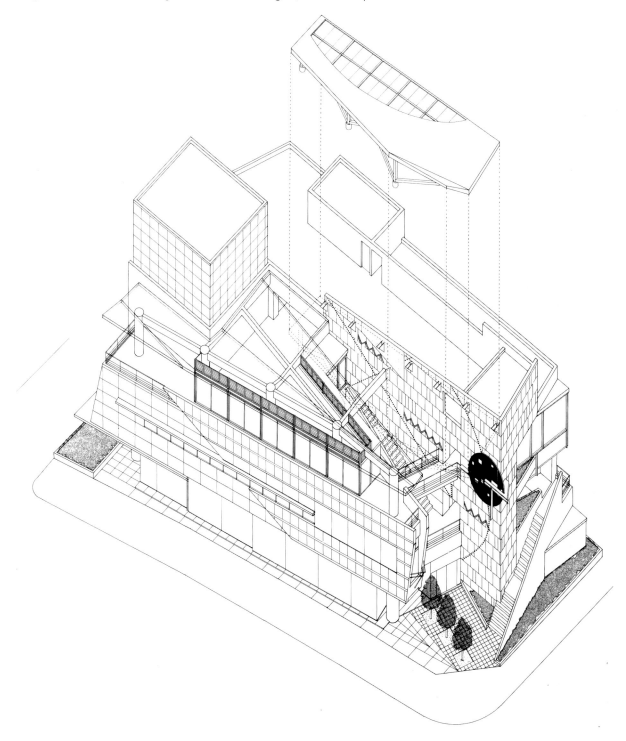

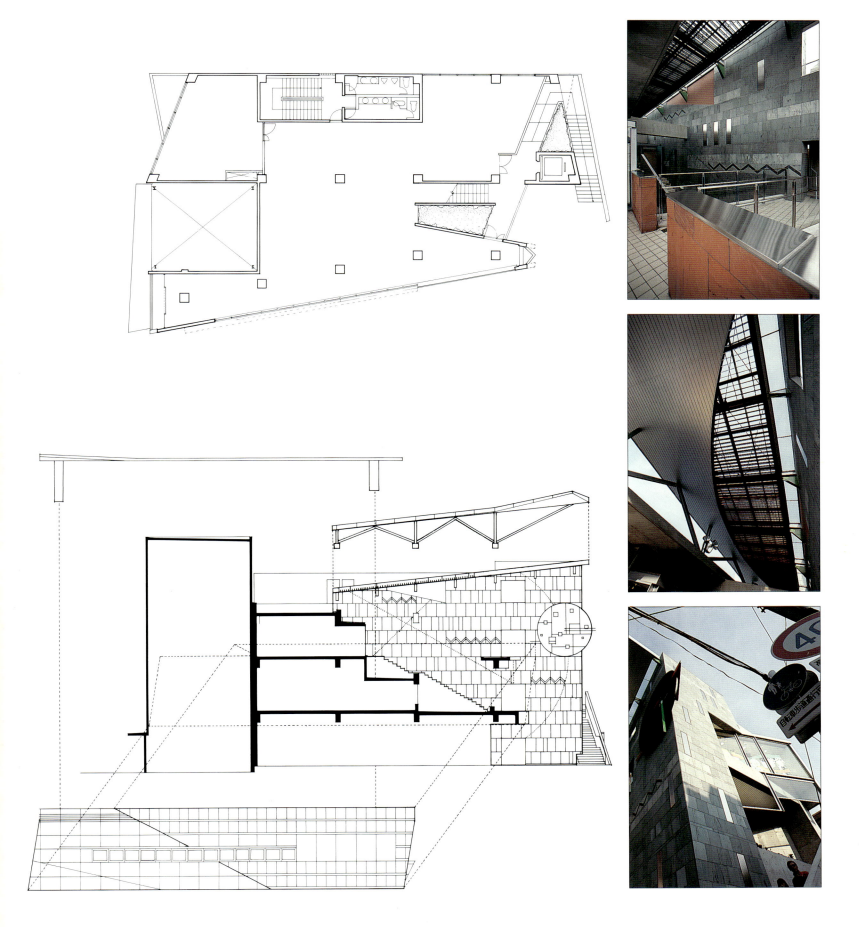

SHOEI YOH
SAIBU GAS MUSEUM OF PHENOMENART, FUKUOKA

Any building under construction looks always beautiful to me because the structure is the first and last element composing the space. Structure is logical and scientific rather than sentimental.

Being ignorant of structural theory, I have enjoyed and utilised modelmaking to find the rules of forces and the surprising laws of nature. The most pleasing structure for me to see, is the one which does not look too strong. I have designed transparent structures in glass such as the WXYZ chairs and a Stainless-steel House with a Light Lattice.

In this Museum, the structural system complemented by a media show of light and sound endow the building with a feeling of lightness. A central void space called the 'Media Space' is surrounded by service walls which are both mechanical and structural, and which are covered by acrylic as well as perforated aluminium panels to both hide and reveal the innumerable sources and kinds of light behind. In order to liberate the area around the receding first floor, the second, third floors and roof slabs are suspended from outside supports. From a slope surrounding the void and from the two bridges above, the audience can look down through the glass surface of the first floor at a co-generation system in the basement, highlighted by illuminating in various ways, during exhibitions.

The sloped galleries around the 'Media Space' contain exhibitions of selected art works based on various physical phenomena, all of which produce, as the general feature of the museum, what I call 'Phenomenart'.

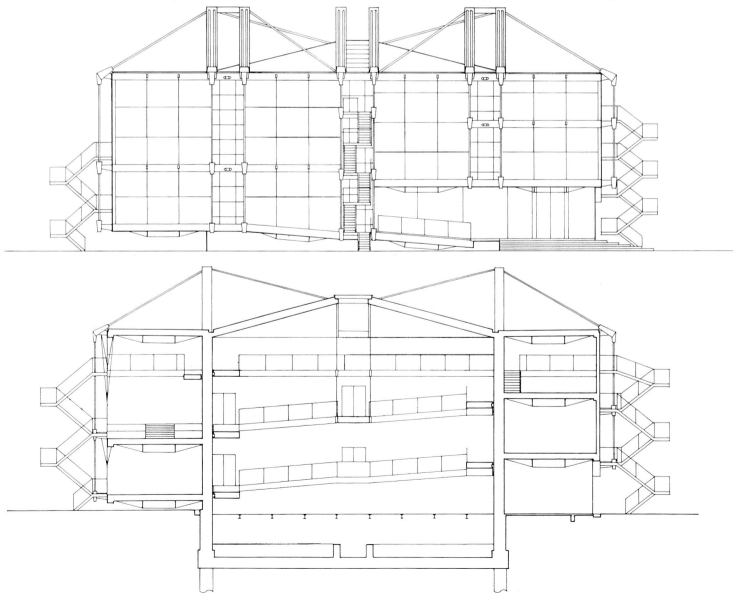

KAZUYO SEJIMA
PLATFORM II, KITAGOMA-GUN, YAMANASHI PREFECTURE

This is a 20-tsubo (720 square feet) studio built at the foot of Mount Yatsugatake. Because this building was to be something like a single-room photo studio/weekend house, and due to the budget allowance, the only available clues to its design requirements were the kitchen and sanitary facilities. I considered these facilities as the only definite components of the building; I made them independent then tried to combine them to make up the whole structure.

Each of the two units was constructed with a system of two glued laminated pieces of timber and a steel ring to connect them. Space for the activities within these facility units was further articulated by adding round steel pipes to the base structures. The introduction of steel truss beams to connect the individual units then established the whole fabric of the building that appears as if intermittently patched together.

The location of each unit was determined by such factors as site conditions, relation to activities, the span of the V-shaped roof deck with small sections, and the distance defined by the size of the truss beams. In addition, in the course of structural assembly, each unit underwent transformation according to its functional need.

All of our Platform I, II, and III projects have various distinctive features in their programming and size, and each one follows a specific architectural agenda. However, one of the underlying themes of II and III has been to extend what was examined in Platform I, ie, how to create locality. The locale produced in each case, I believe, is generally of the same nature, insofar as in all three, a locale that is synchronised with numerous activities, a condition I call *Platform*, has been commonly attempted.

In the process of planning such a building in concrete terms, the question we may come up with is what produces such a locale: I think it is structure. Therefore, I initiated the plans for all of Platforms I, II, and III with structure. First of all, structures were studied not merely in a sense of dynamics, but rather as a framework closely related to specific activities. This way a certain area became defined. As a result, some planes and sections came forth. Each completed structure was arranged so as to fit the site restrictions and functional requirements. Sometimes the shape itself was modified and altered. Next they were connected to one another in a practical manner until finally a structure was accomplished. Such a structure features a curious, ambiguous quality insofar as it is difficult to decide whether one is dealing with a complete entity that is a whole in itself, or only a part, that is only a fragment of a larger whole.

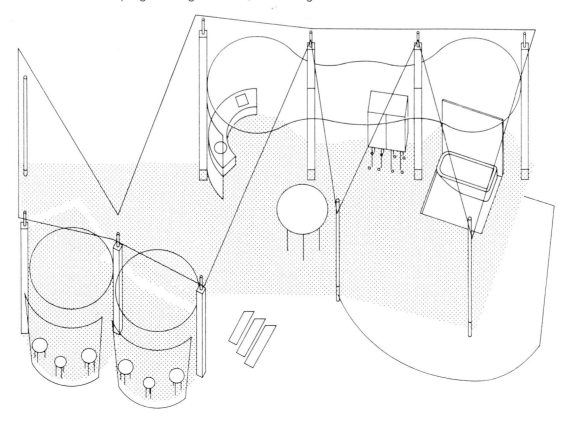